THE CLONE WARS™

DEFENDERS OF THE LOST TEMPLE

DESIGNER **KRYSTAL HENNES**

ASSISTANT EDITOR **FREDDYE LINS**

EDITOR **DAVE MARSHALL**

PUBLISHER **MIKE RICHARDSON**

Special thanks to Joanne Chan Taylor, Leland Chee, Troy Alders, Carol Roeder, Jann Moorhead, and David Anderman at Lucas Licensing.

Published by Dark Horse Books, a division of Dark Horse Comics, Inc.
10956 SE Main Street, Milwaukie, OR 97222

DarkHorse.com | StarWars.com

To find a comics shop in your area, call the Comic Shop Locator Service toll-free at 1.888.266.4226
First edition: March 2013 | ISBN 978-1-61655-058-5

10 9 8 7 6 5 4 3 2 1

Printed in China

Library of Congress Cataloging-in-Publication Data

Aclin, Justin.
Star Wars, the clone wars. Defenders of the lost temple / script, Justin Aclin ; art, Ben Bates ; colors, Michael Atiyeh ; lettering, Michael Heisler ; cover art, Mike Hawthorne. -- 1st ed.
    p. cm.
Summary: On a mission with a Jedi general, one clone trooper discovers who he is and where he came from when a group of the warrior Mandalorians appear.
ISBN 978-1-61655-058-5
1. Star Wars fiction. 2. Extraterrestrial beings--Comic books, strips, etc. 3. Extraterrestrial beings--Juvenile fiction. 4. Space warfare--Comic books, strips, etc. 5. Space warfare--Juvenile fiction. 6. Graphic novels. [1. Graphic novels. 2. Extraterrestrial beings--Fiction. 3. Space warfare--Fiction.] I. Bates, Ben, 1982- ill. II. Hawthorne, Mike, ill. III. Title. IV. Title: Defenders of the lost temple.
PZ7.7.A28Sth 2013
741.5'973--dc23
                                    2012040395

STAR WARS

THE CLONE WARS

DEFENDERS OF THE LOST TEMPLE

SCRIPT **JUSTIN ACLIN**   ART **BEN BATES**

COLORS **MICHAEL ATIYEH**   LETTERING **MICHAEL HEISLER**

COVER ART **MIKE HAWTHORNE**

DARK HORSE BOOKS

LUCAS BOOKS

This story takes place sometime between seasons 4 and 5 of *The Clone Wars*.

INFINITIES

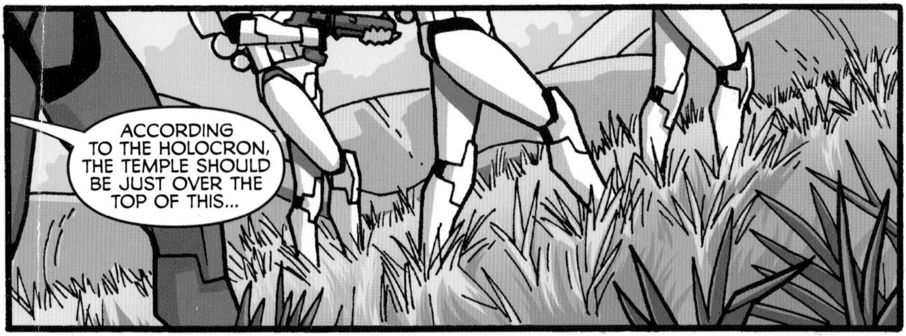
ACCORDING TO THE HOLOCRON, THE TEMPLE SHOULD BE JUST OVER THE TOP OF THIS...

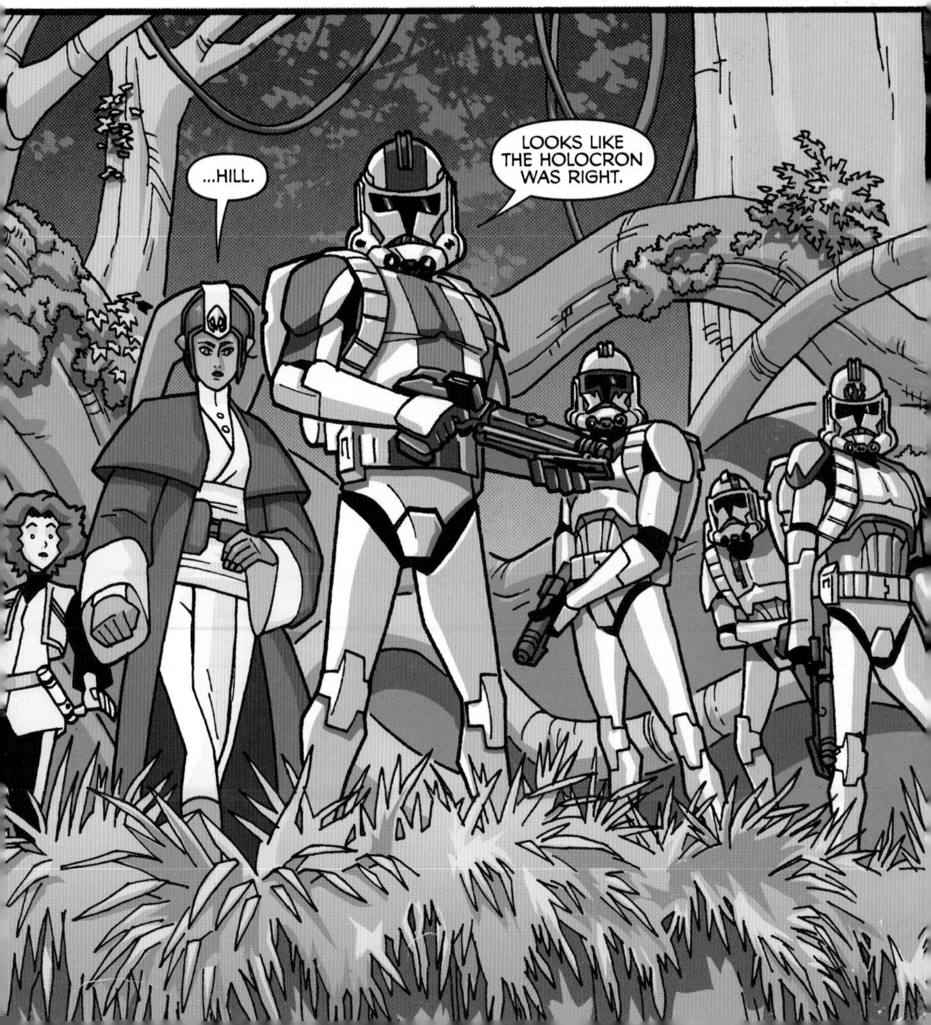
...HILL.
LOOKS LIKE THE HOLOCRON WAS RIGHT.

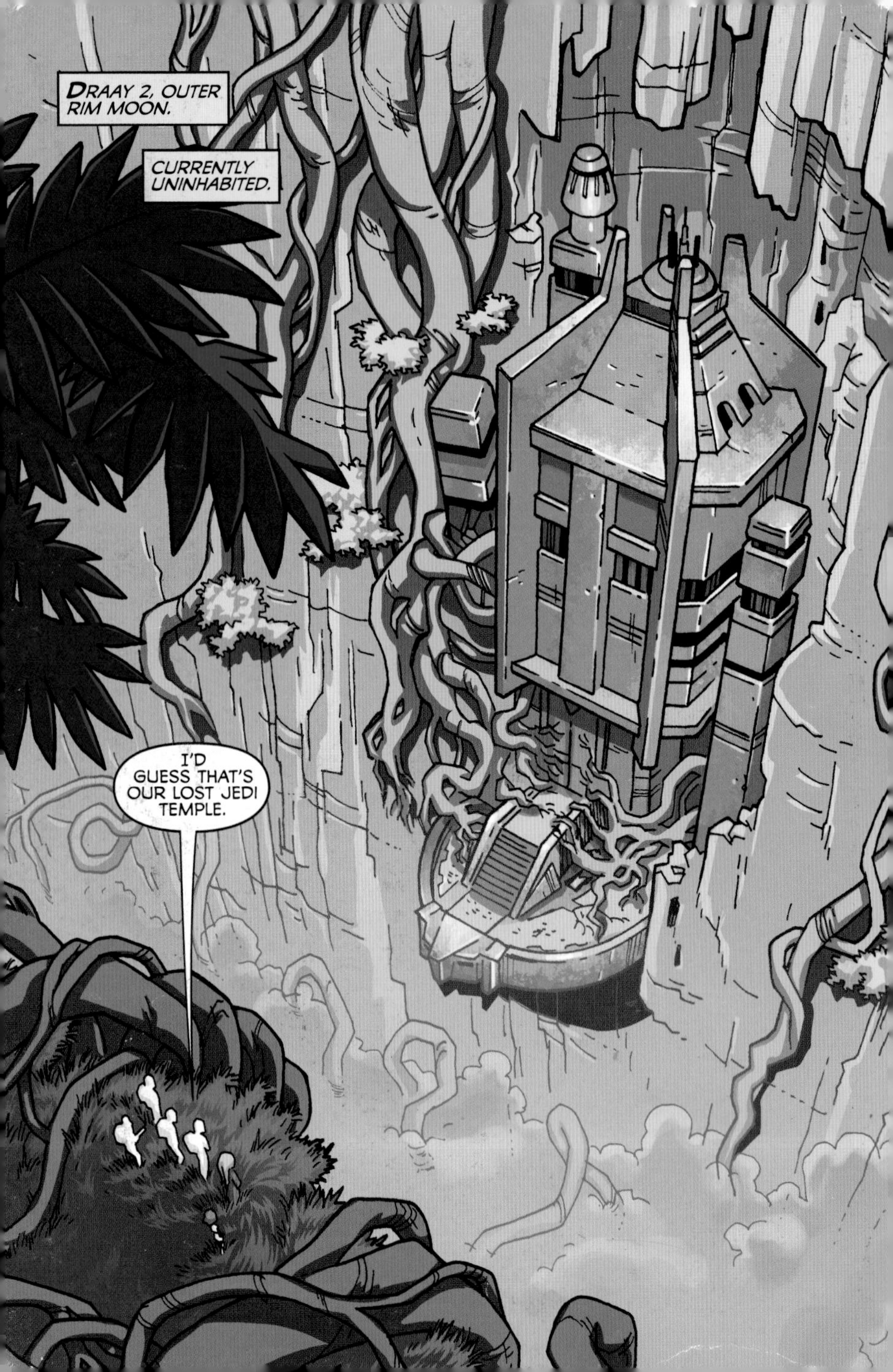
DRAAY 2, OUTER RIM MOON.
CURRENTLY UNINHABITED.
I'D GUESS THAT'S OUR LOST JEDI TEMPLE.

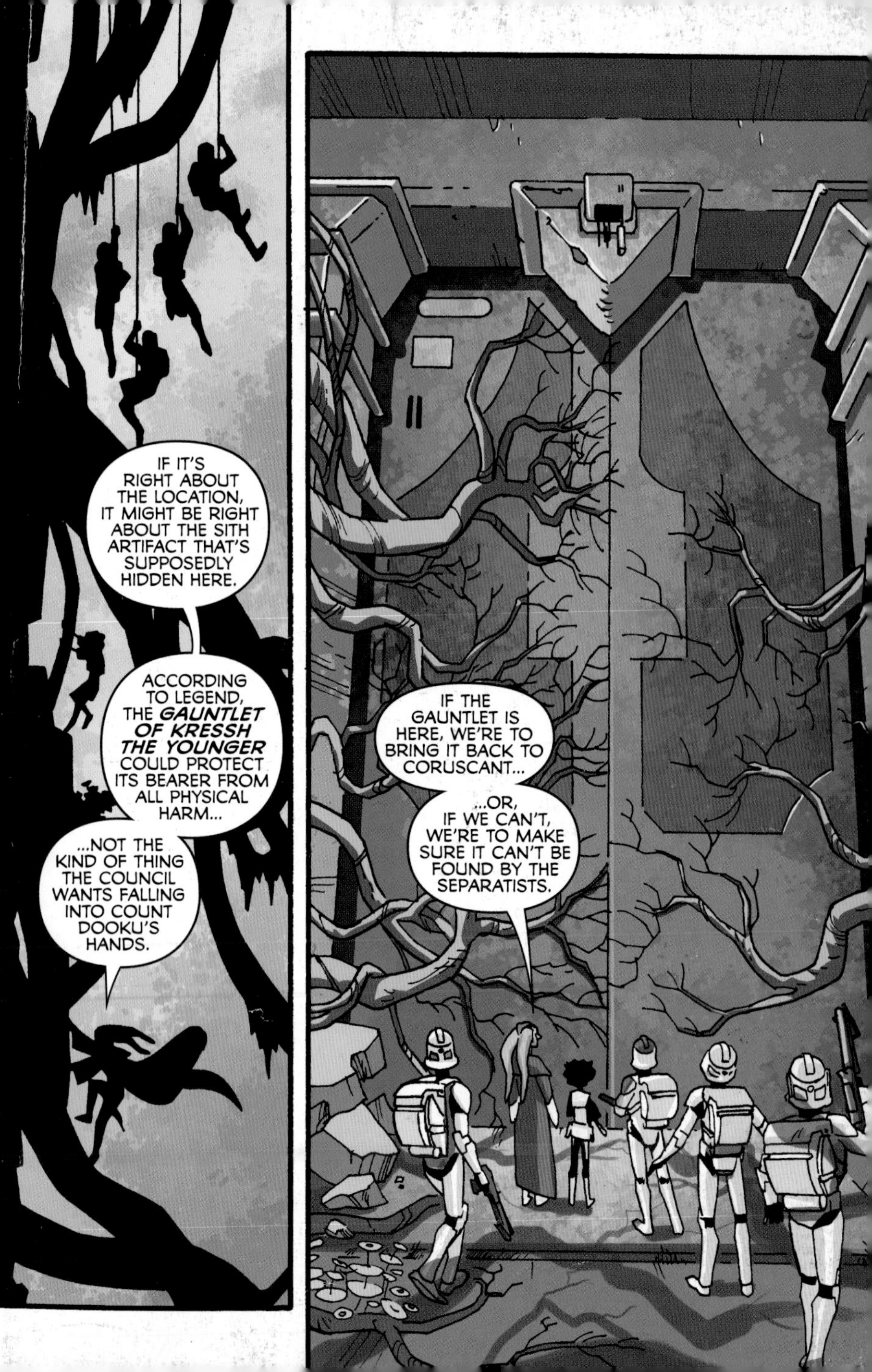
IF IT'S RIGHT ABOUT THE LOCATION, IT MIGHT BE RIGHT ABOUT THE SITH ARTIFACT THAT'S SUPPOSEDLY HIDDEN HERE.
ACCORDING TO LEGEND, THE ***GAUNTLET OF KRESSH THE YOUNGER*** COULD PROTECT ITS BEARER FROM ALL PHYSICAL HARM...
...NOT THE KIND OF THING THE COUNCIL WANTS FALLING INTO COUNT DOOKU'S HANDS.
IF THE GAUNTLET IS HERE, WE'RE TO BRING IT BACK TO CORUSCANT...
...OR, IF WE CAN'T, WE'RE TO MAKE SURE IT CAN'T BE FOUND BY THE SEPARATISTS.

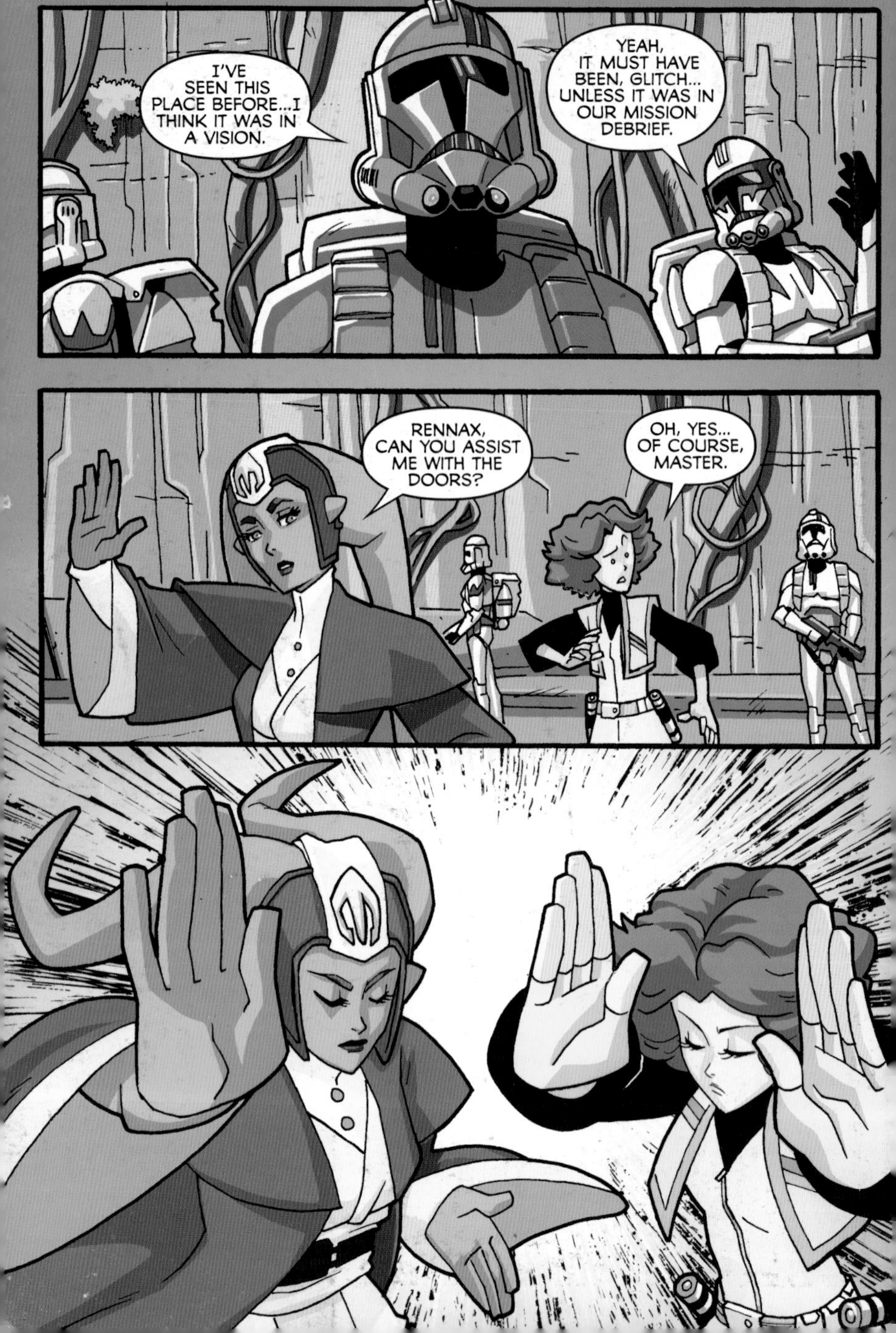
I'VE SEEN THIS PLACE BEFORE...I THINK IT WAS IN A VISION.
YEAH, IT MUST HAVE BEEN, GLITCH... UNLESS IT WAS IN OUR MISSION DEBRIEF.
RENNAX, CAN YOU ASSIST ME WITH THE DOORS?
OH, YES... OF COURSE, MASTER.

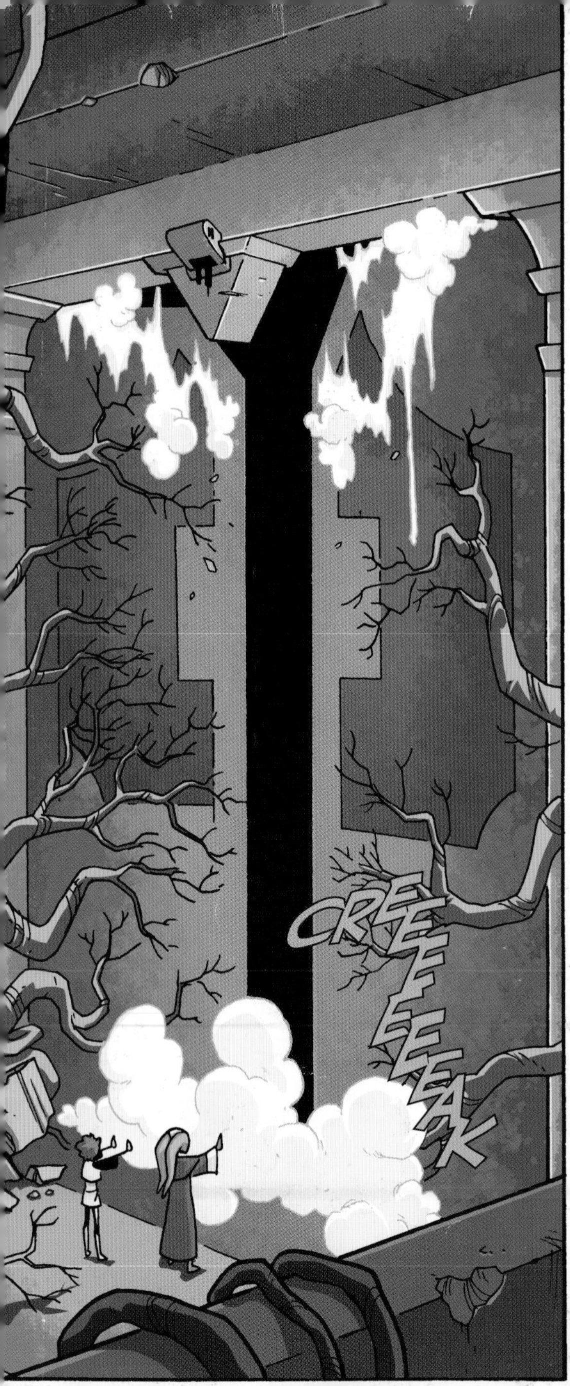
CREEEEEEAK

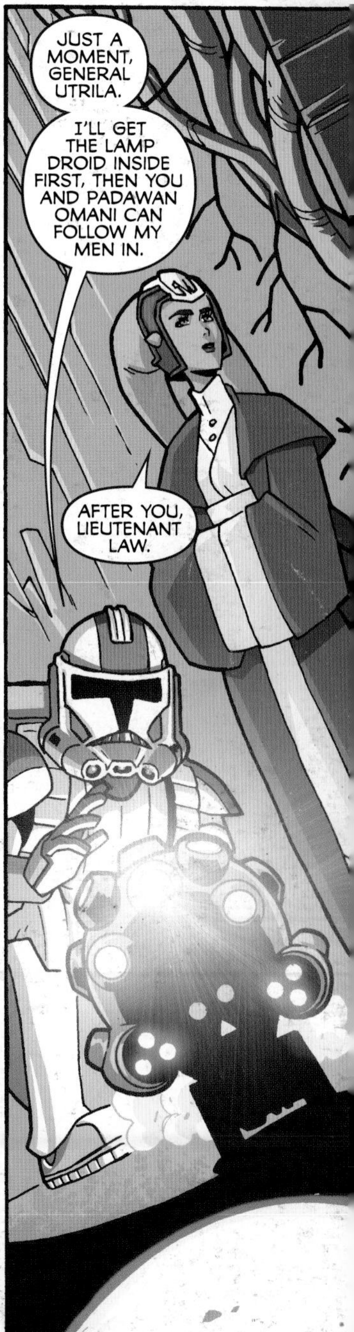
JUST A MOMENT, GENERAL UTRILA.
I'LL GET THE LAMP DROID INSIDE FIRST, THEN YOU AND PADAWAN OMANI CAN FOLLOW MY MEN IN.
AFTER YOU, LIEUTENANT LAW.

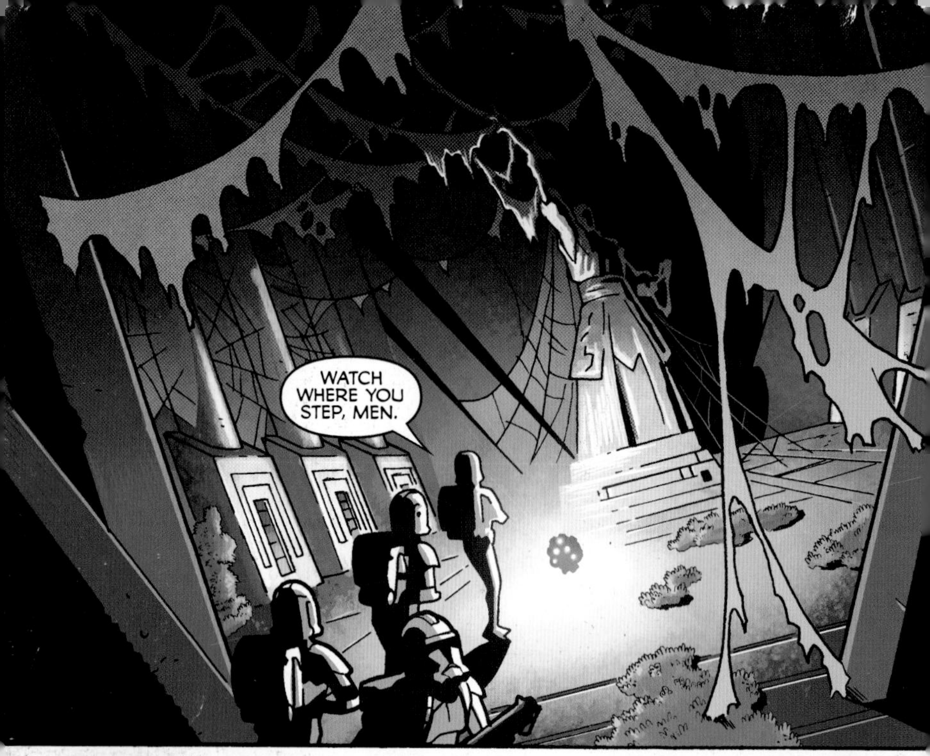
WATCH WHERE YOU STEP, MEN.

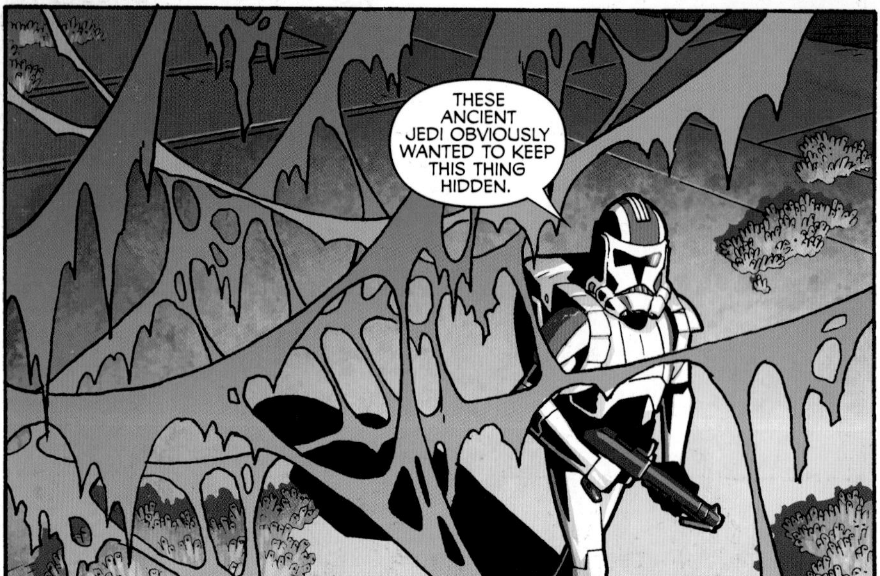
THESE ANCIENT JEDI OBVIOUSLY WANTED TO KEEP THIS THING HIDDEN.

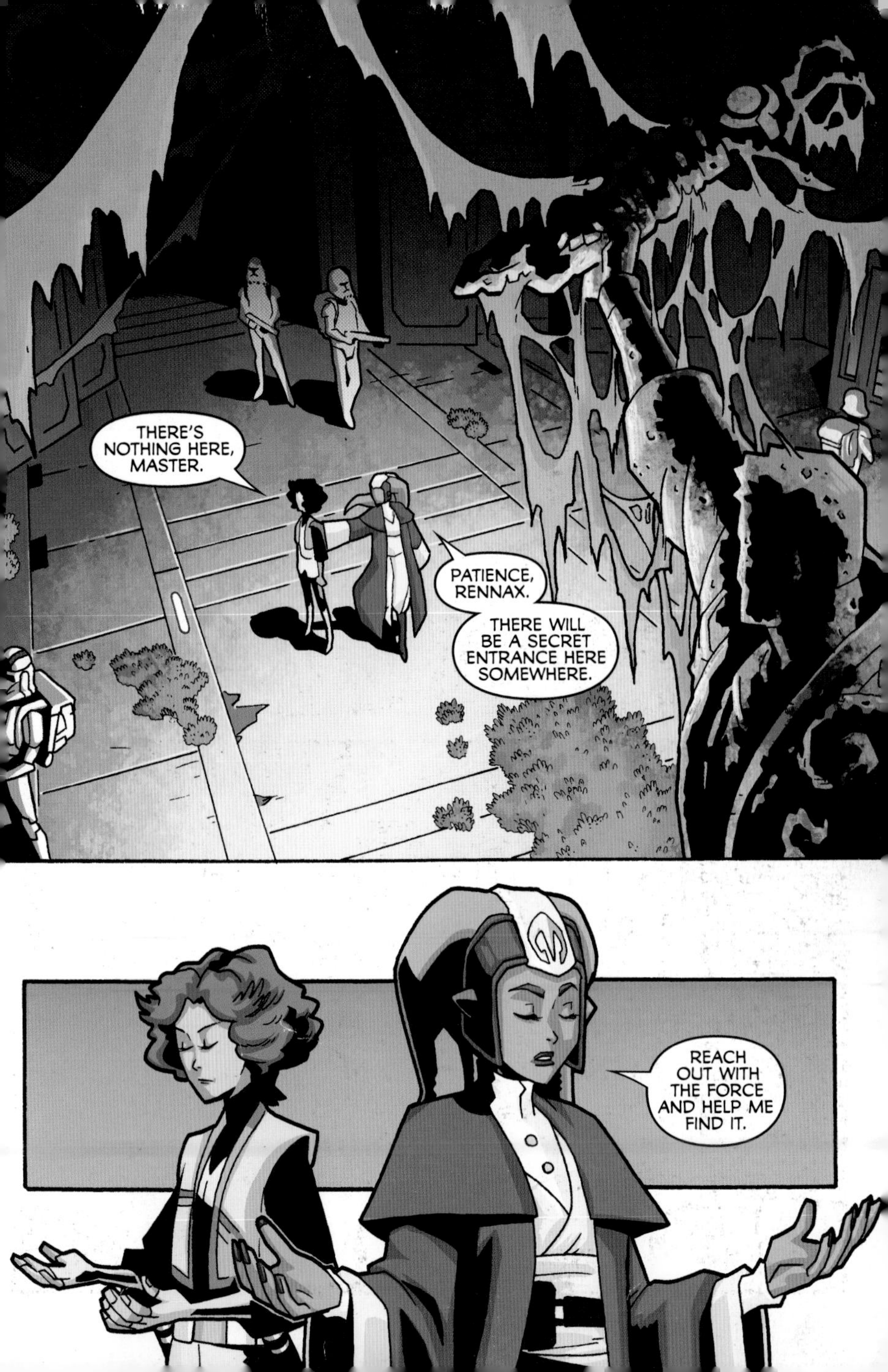
THERE'S NOTHING HERE, MASTER.
PATIENCE, RENNAX.
THERE WILL BE A SECRET ENTRANCE HERE SOMEWHERE.
REACH OUT WITH THE FORCE AND HELP ME FIND IT.

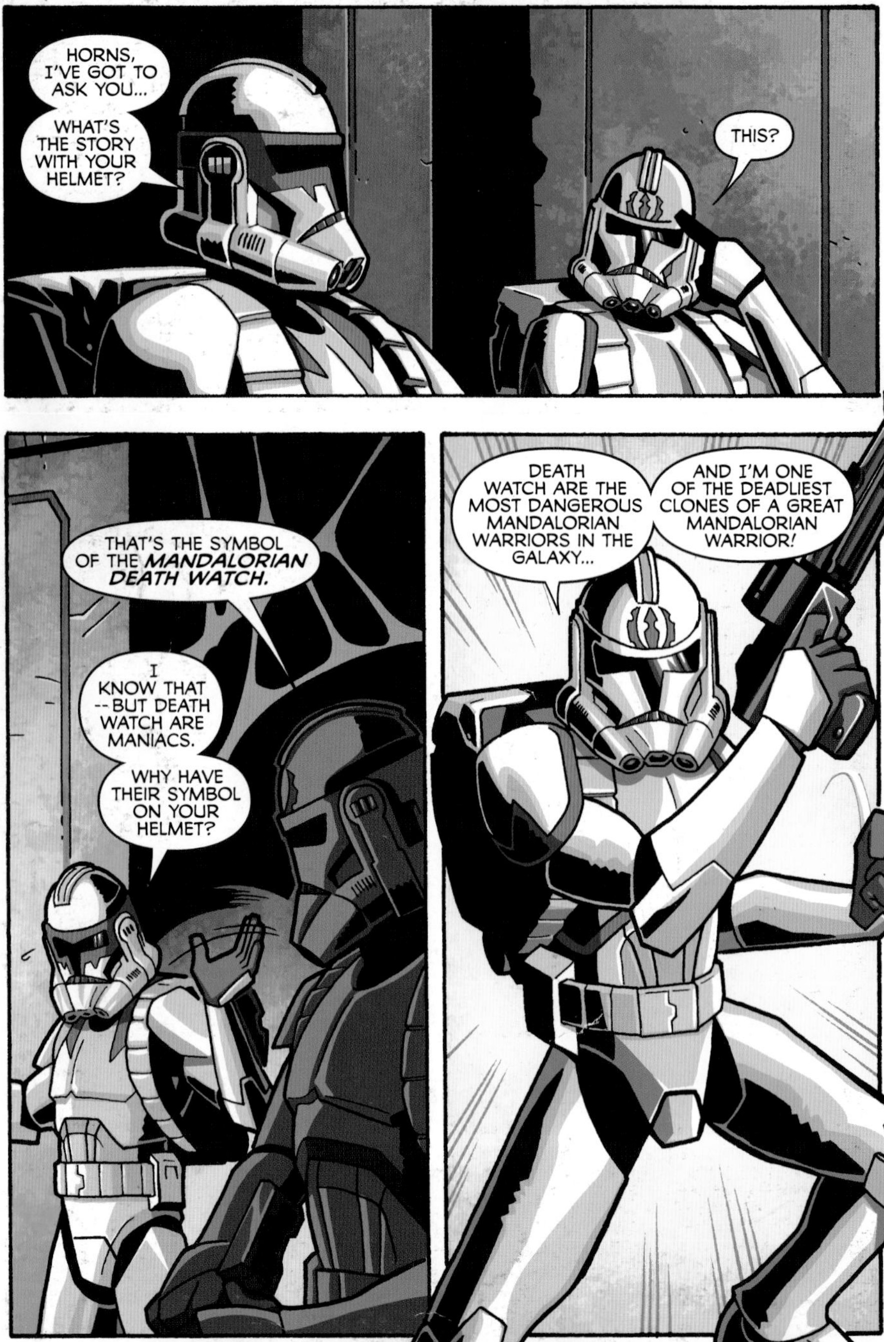
HORNS, I'VE GOT TO ASK YOU...
WHAT'S THE STORY WITH YOUR HELMET?
THIS?
THAT'S THE SYMBOL OF THE *MANDALORIAN DEATH WATCH.*
I KNOW THAT -- BUT DEATH WATCH ARE MANIACS.
WHY HAVE THEIR SYMBOL ON YOUR HELMET?
DEATH WATCH ARE THE MOST DANGEROUS MANDALORIAN WARRIORS IN THE GALAXY...
AND I'M ONE OF THE DEADLIEST CLONES OF A GREAT MANDALORIAN WARRIOR!

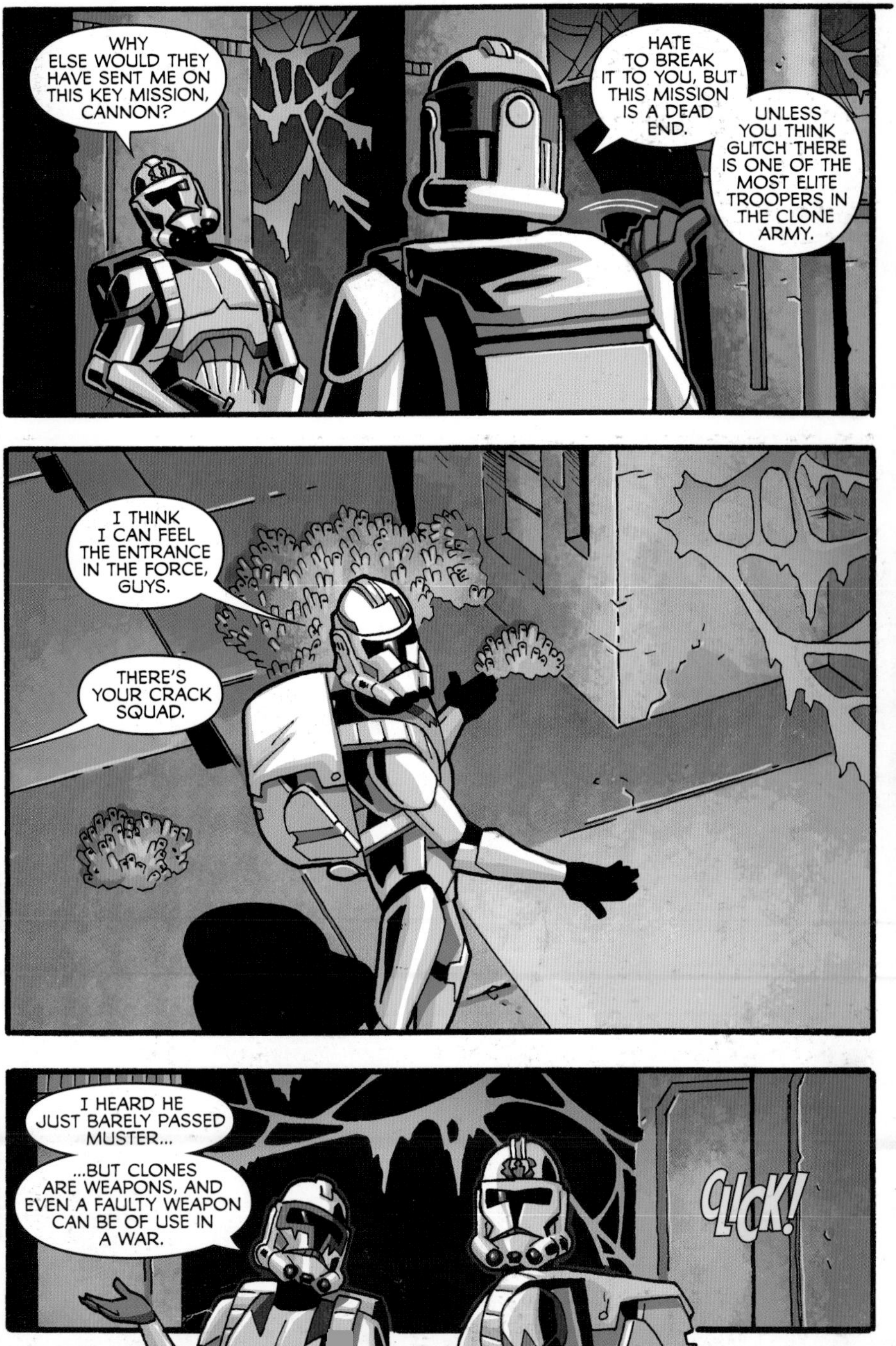
WHY ELSE WOULD THEY HAVE SENT ME ON THIS KEY MISSION, CANNON?
HATE TO BREAK IT TO YOU, BUT THIS MISSION IS A DEAD END.
UNLESS YOU THINK GLITCH THERE IS ONE OF THE MOST ELITE TROOPERS IN THE CLONE ARMY.
I THINK I CAN FEEL THE ENTRANCE IN THE FORCE, GUYS.
THERE'S YOUR CRACK SQUAD.
I HEARD HE JUST BARELY PASSED MUSTER...
...BUT CLONES ARE WEAPONS, AND EVEN A FAULTY WEAPON CAN BE OF USE IN A WAR.
CLICK!

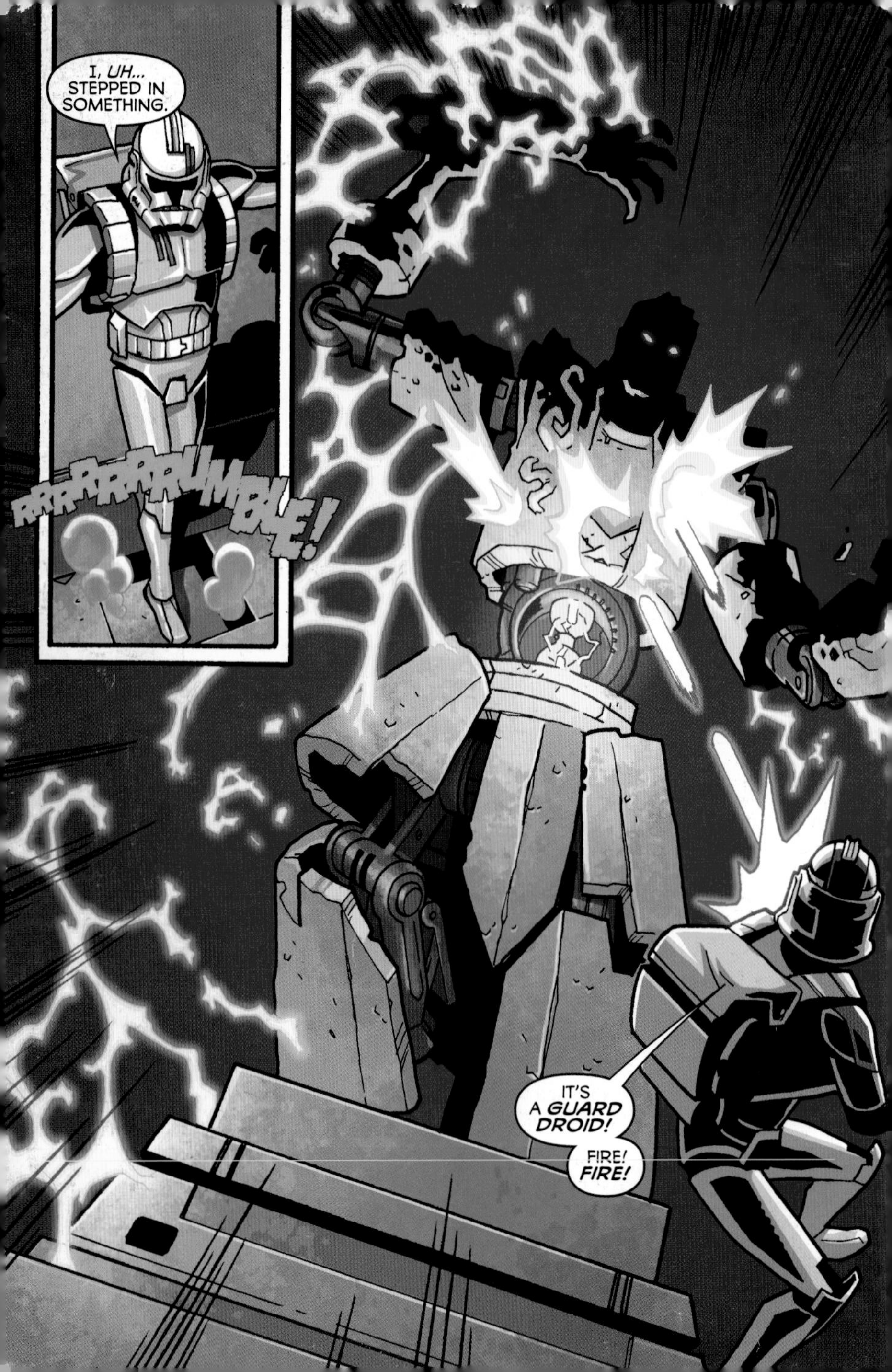
I, UH... STEPPED IN SOMETHING.
RRRRRRRRRUMBLE!
IT'S A GUARD DROID!
FIRE! FIRE!

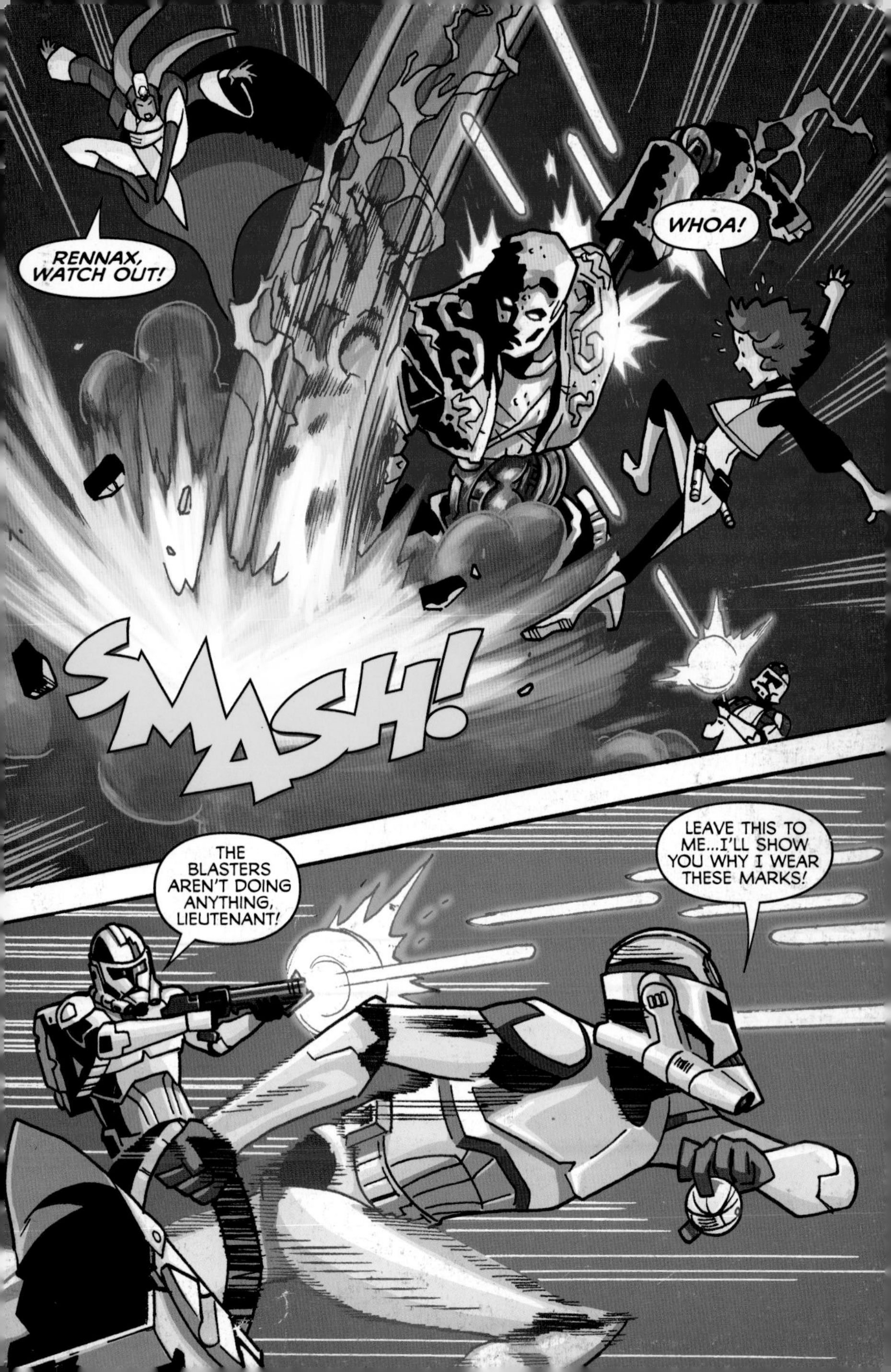
RENNAX, WATCH OUT!
WHOA!
SMASH!
THE BLASTERS AREN'T DOING ANYTHING, LIEUTENANT!
LEAVE THIS TO ME...I'LL SHOW YOU WHY I WEAR THESE MARKS!

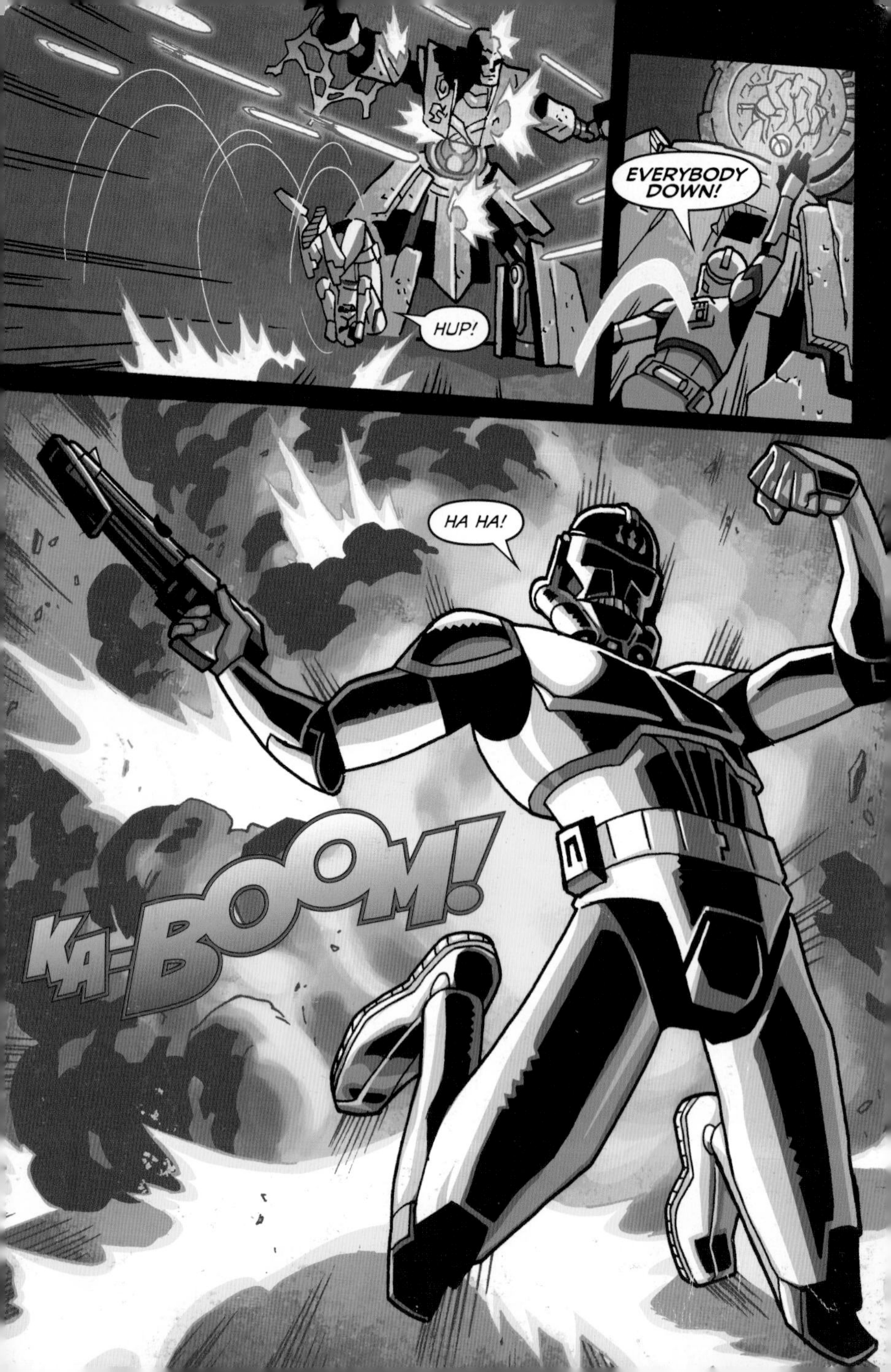
EVERYBODY DOWN!
HUP!
HA HA!
KA-BOOM!

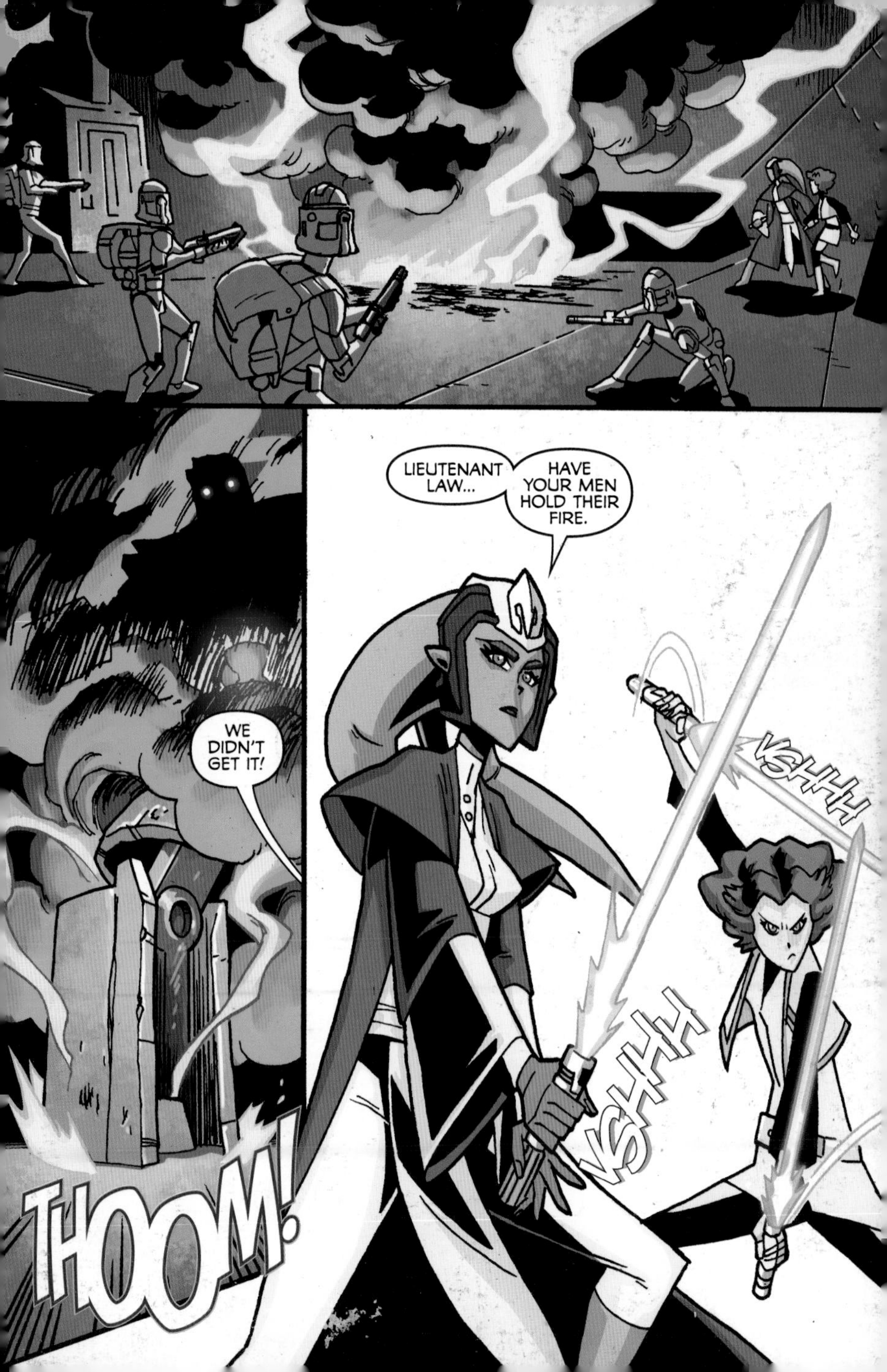
WE DIDN'T GET IT!
THOOM!
LIEUTENANT LAW...
HAVE YOUR MEN HOLD THEIR FIRE.
VSHHH
VSHHH

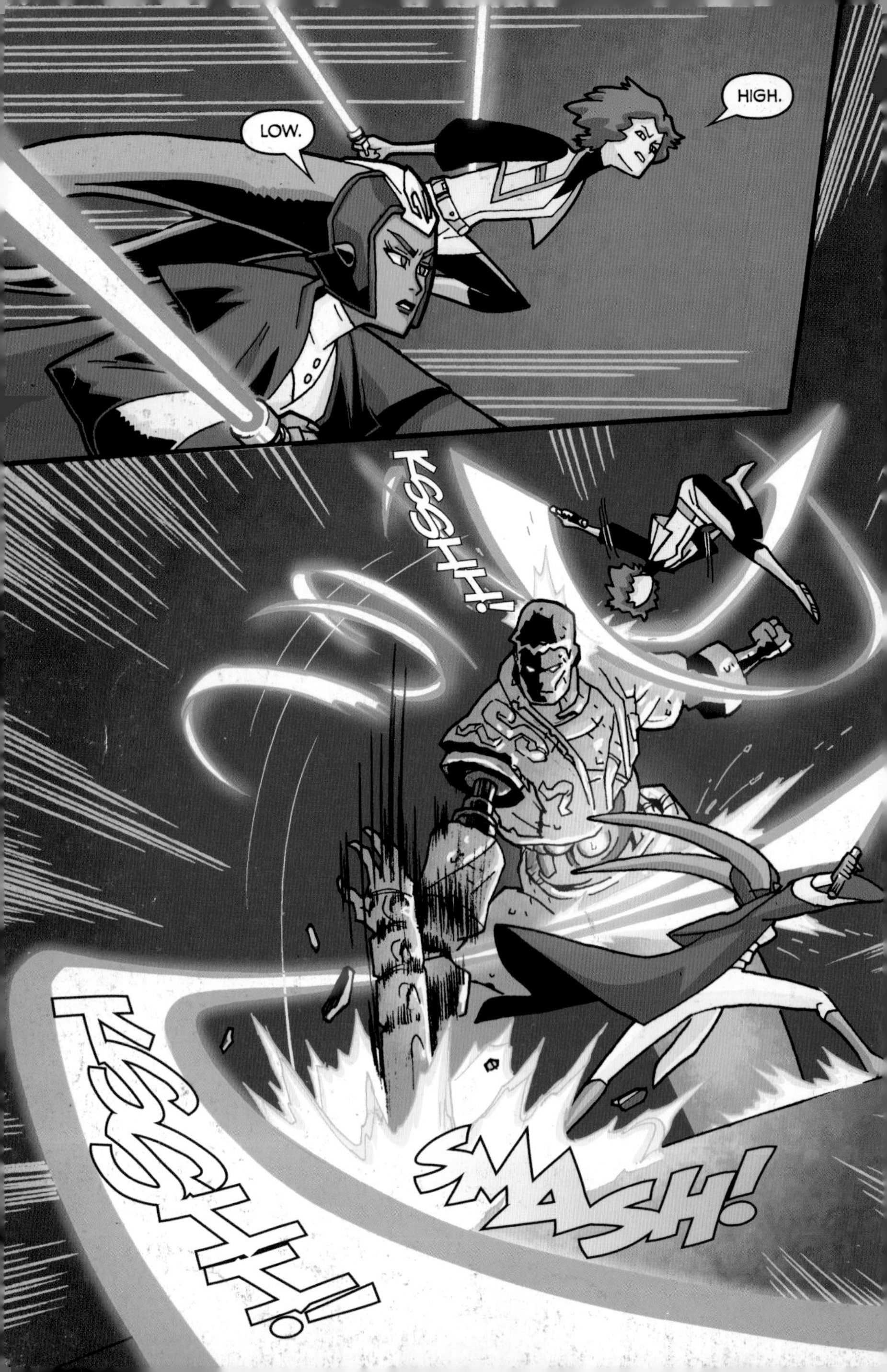
LOW.
HIGH.
KSSHH!
KSSHH!
SMASH!

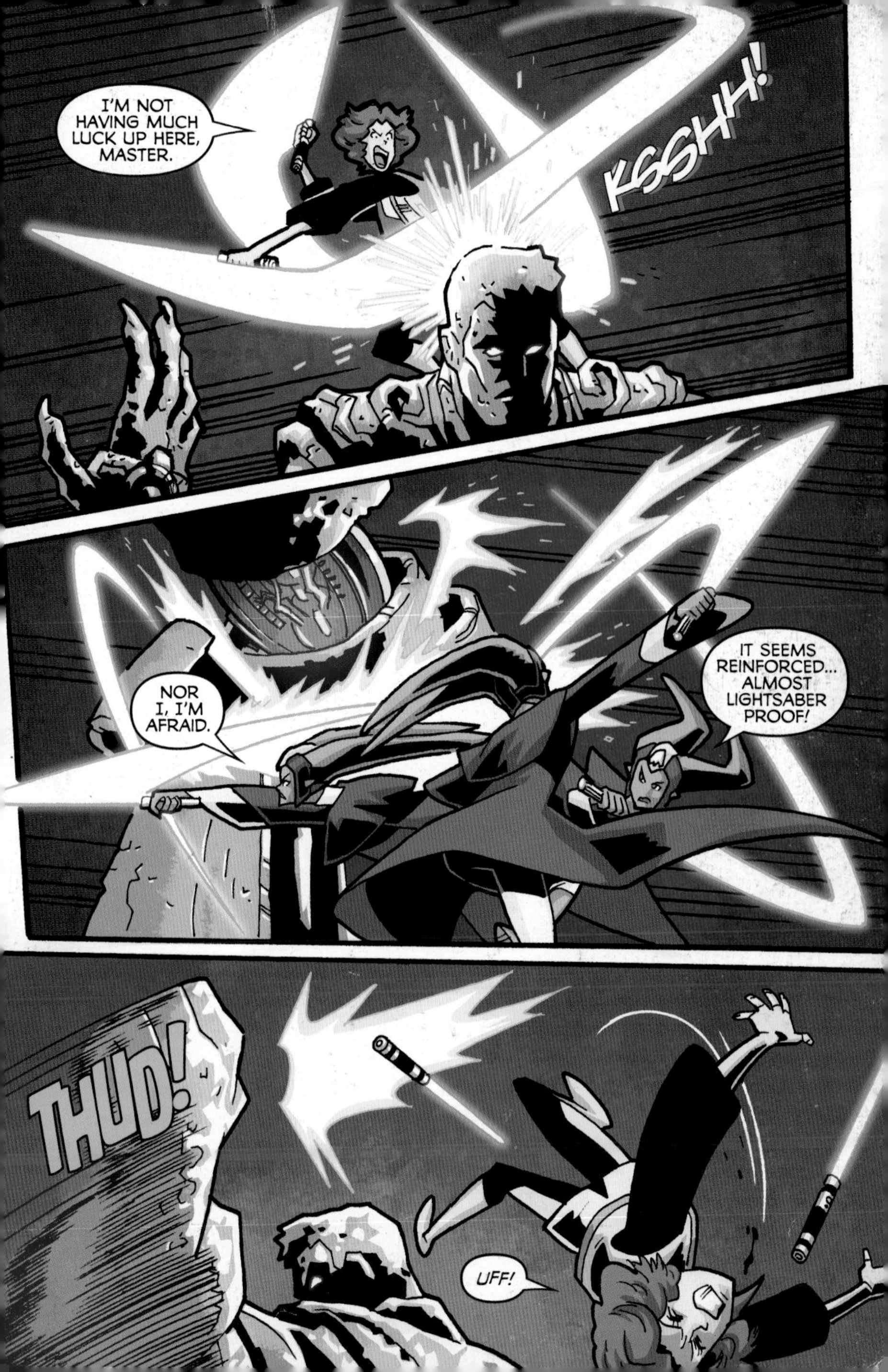

I'M NOT HAVING MUCH LUCK UP HERE, MASTER.
KSSHH!
NOR I, I'M AFRAID.
IT SEEMS REINFORCED... ALMOST LIGHTSABER PROOF!
THUD!
UFF!

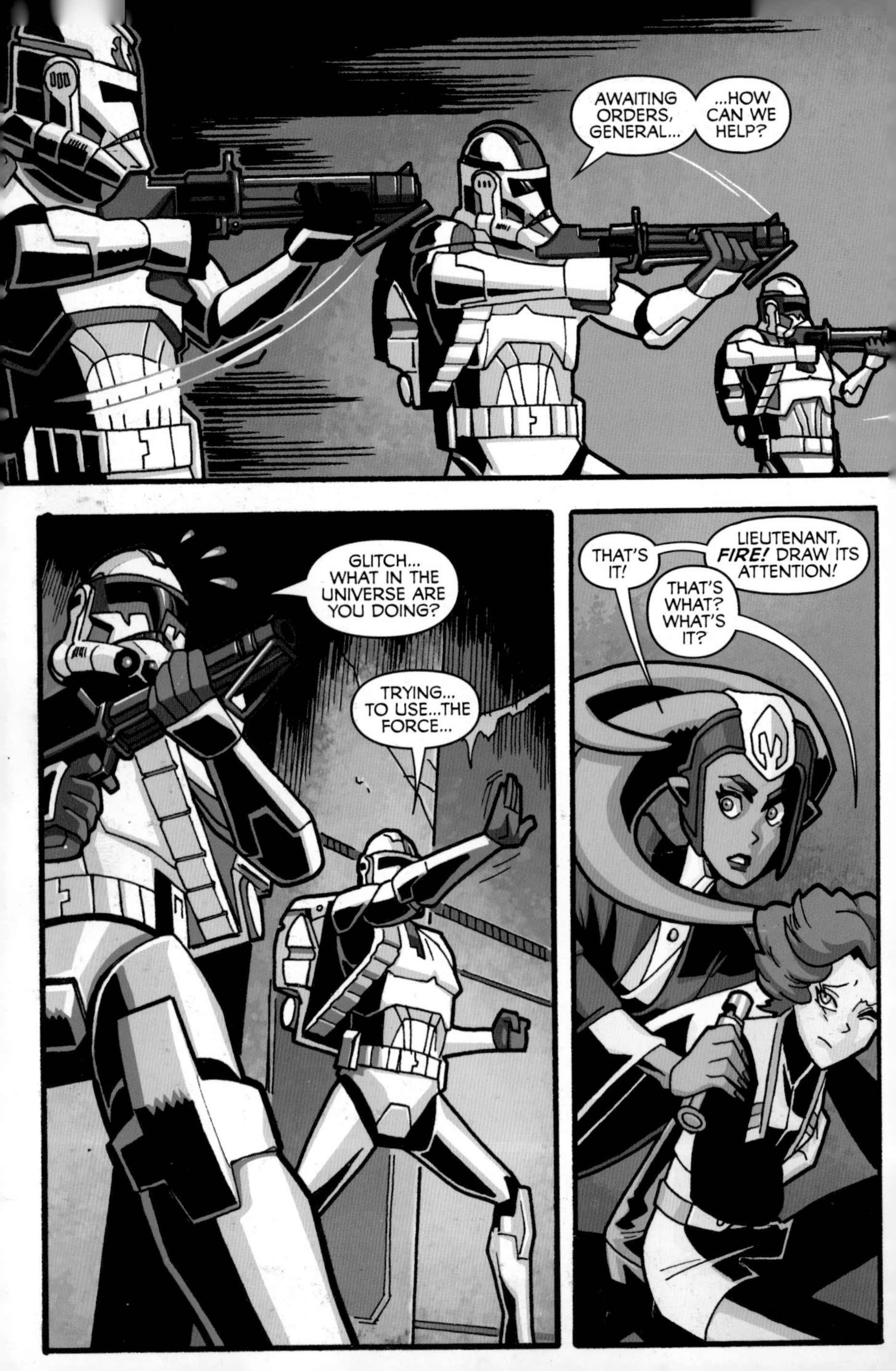
AWAITING ORDERS, GENERAL...
...HOW CAN WE HELP?
GLITCH... WHAT IN THE UNIVERSE ARE YOU DOING?
TRYING... TO USE...THE FORCE...
THAT'S IT!
LIEUTENANT, FIRE! DRAW ITS ATTENTION!
THAT'S WHAT? WHAT'S IT?

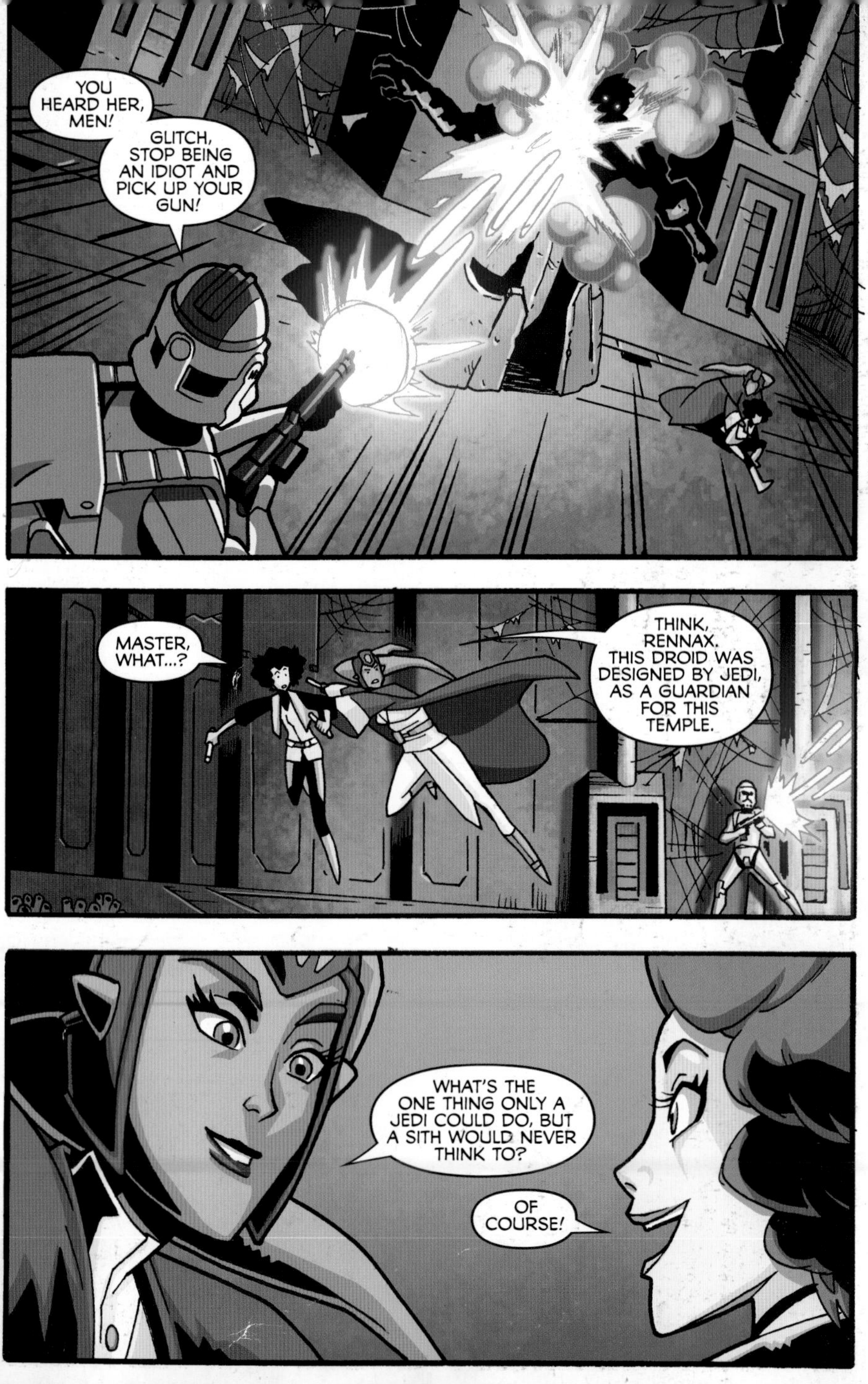
YOU HEARD HER, MEN!
GLITCH, STOP BEING AN IDIOT AND PICK UP YOUR GUN!
MASTER, WHAT...?
THINK, RENNAX. THIS DROID WAS DESIGNED BY JEDI, AS A GUARDIAN FOR THIS TEMPLE.
WHAT'S THE ONE THING ONLY A JEDI COULD DO, BUT A SITH WOULD NEVER THINK TO?
OF COURSE!

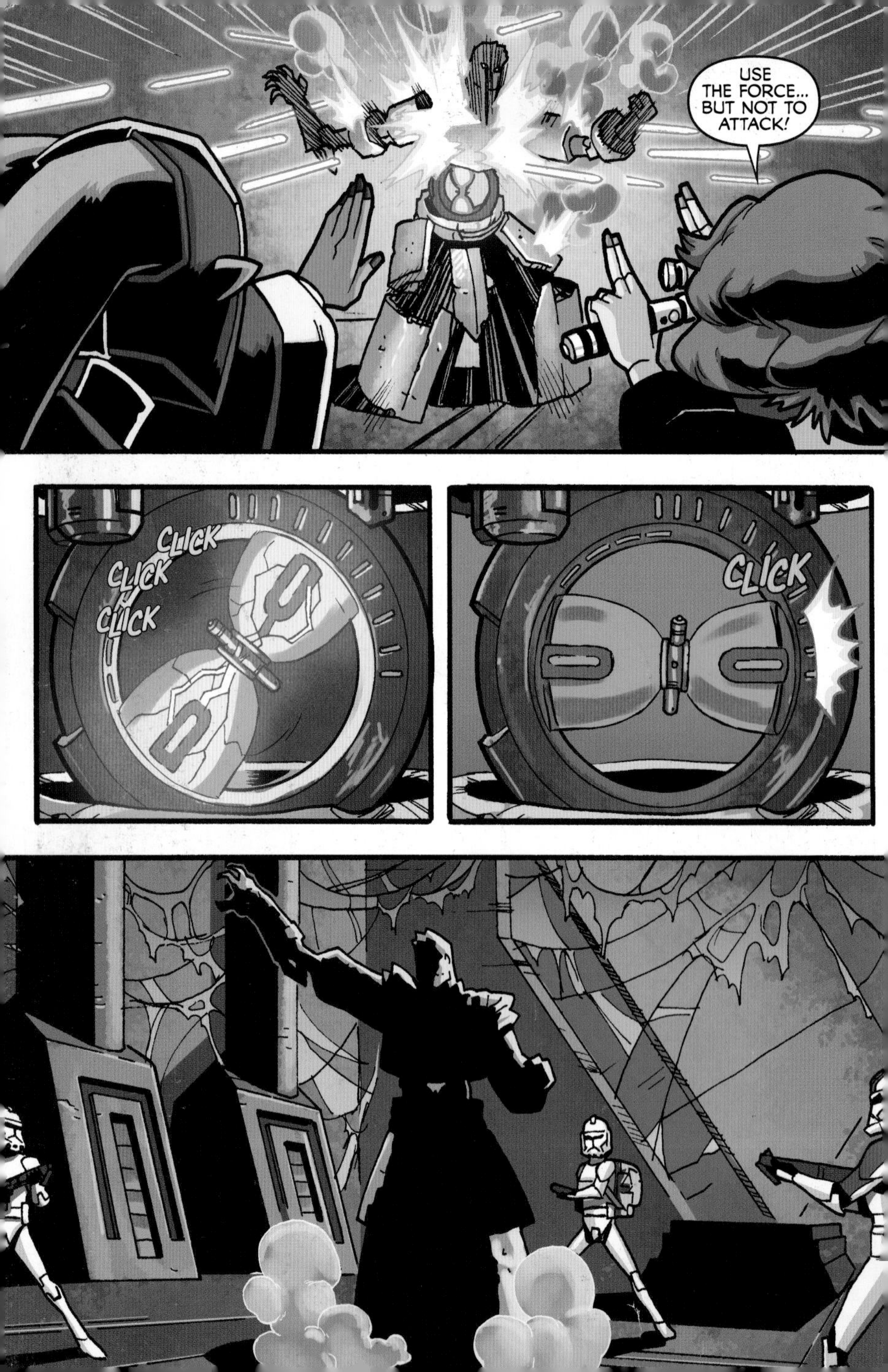
USE THE FORCE... BUT NOT TO ATTACK!
CLICK
CLICK
CLICK
CLICK

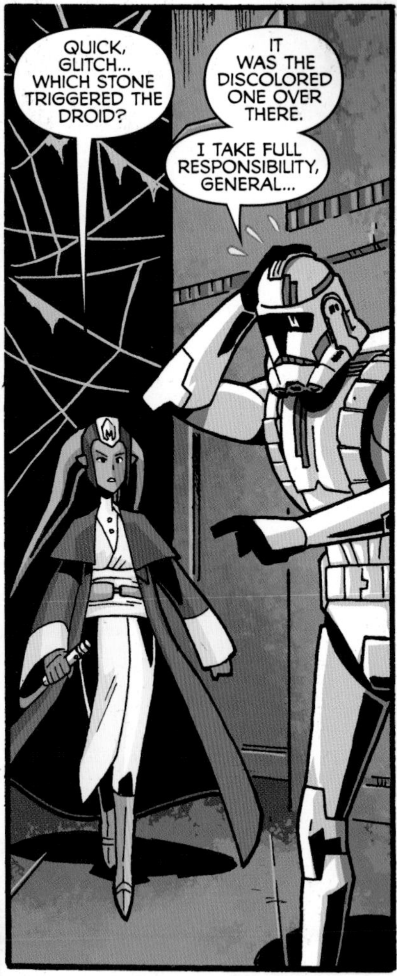
QUICK, GLITCH... WHICH STONE TRIGGERED THE DROID?
IT WAS THE DISCOLORED ONE OVER THERE.
I TAKE FULL RESPONSIBILITY, GENERAL...
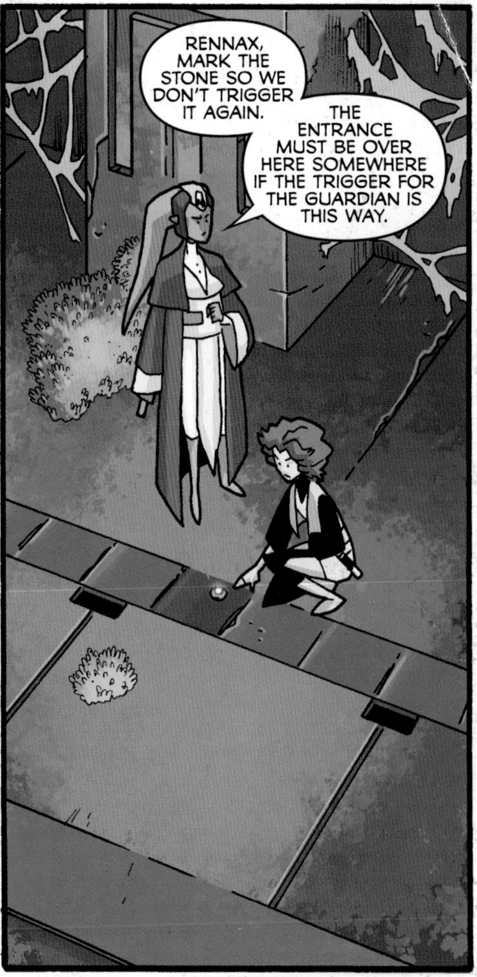
RENNAX, MARK THE STONE SO WE DON'T TRIGGER IT AGAIN.
THE ENTRANCE MUST BE OVER HERE SOMEWHERE IF THE TRIGGER FOR THE GUARDIAN IS THIS WAY.
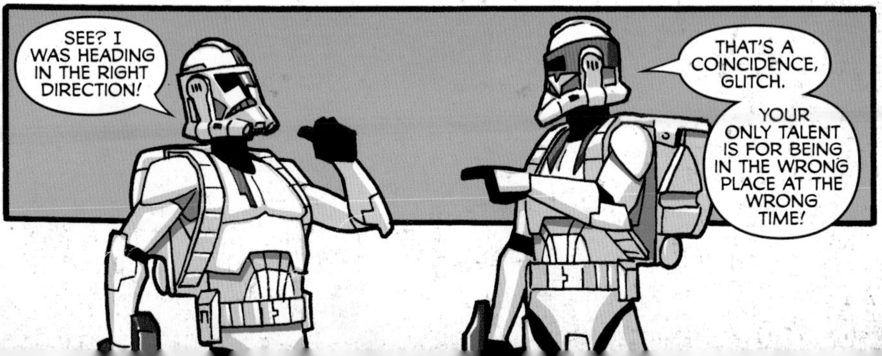
SEE? I WAS HEADING IN THE RIGHT DIRECTION!
THAT'S A COINCIDENCE, GLITCH.
YOUR ONLY TALENT IS FOR BEING IN THE WRONG PLACE AT THE WRONG TIME!

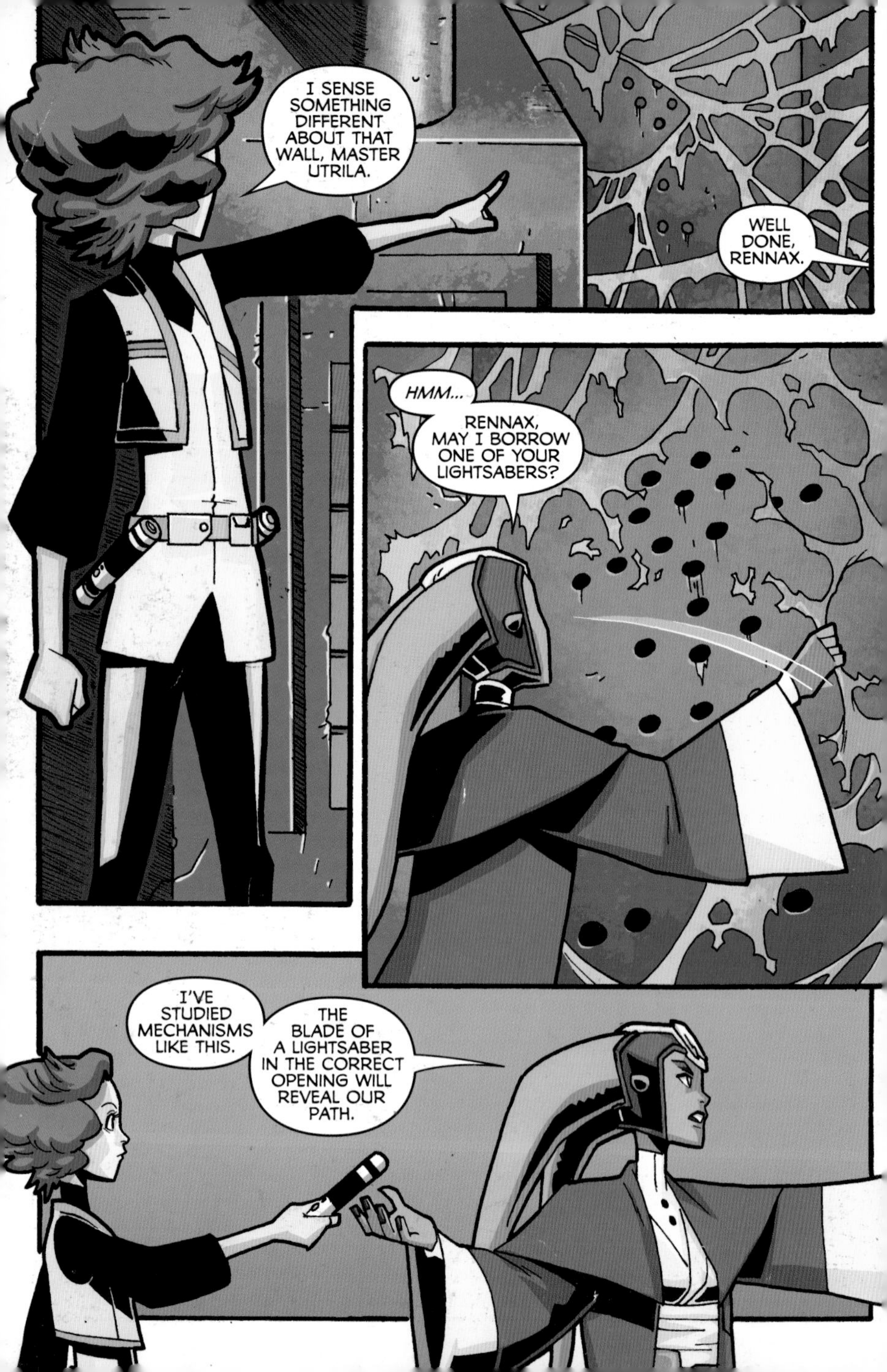
I SENSE SOMETHING DIFFERENT ABOUT THAT WALL, MASTER UTRILA.
WELL DONE, RENNAX.
HMM...
RENNAX, MAY I BORROW ONE OF YOUR LIGHTSABERS?
I'VE STUDIED MECHANISMS LIKE THIS.
THE BLADE OF A LIGHTSABER IN THE CORRECT OPENING WILL REVEAL OUR PATH.

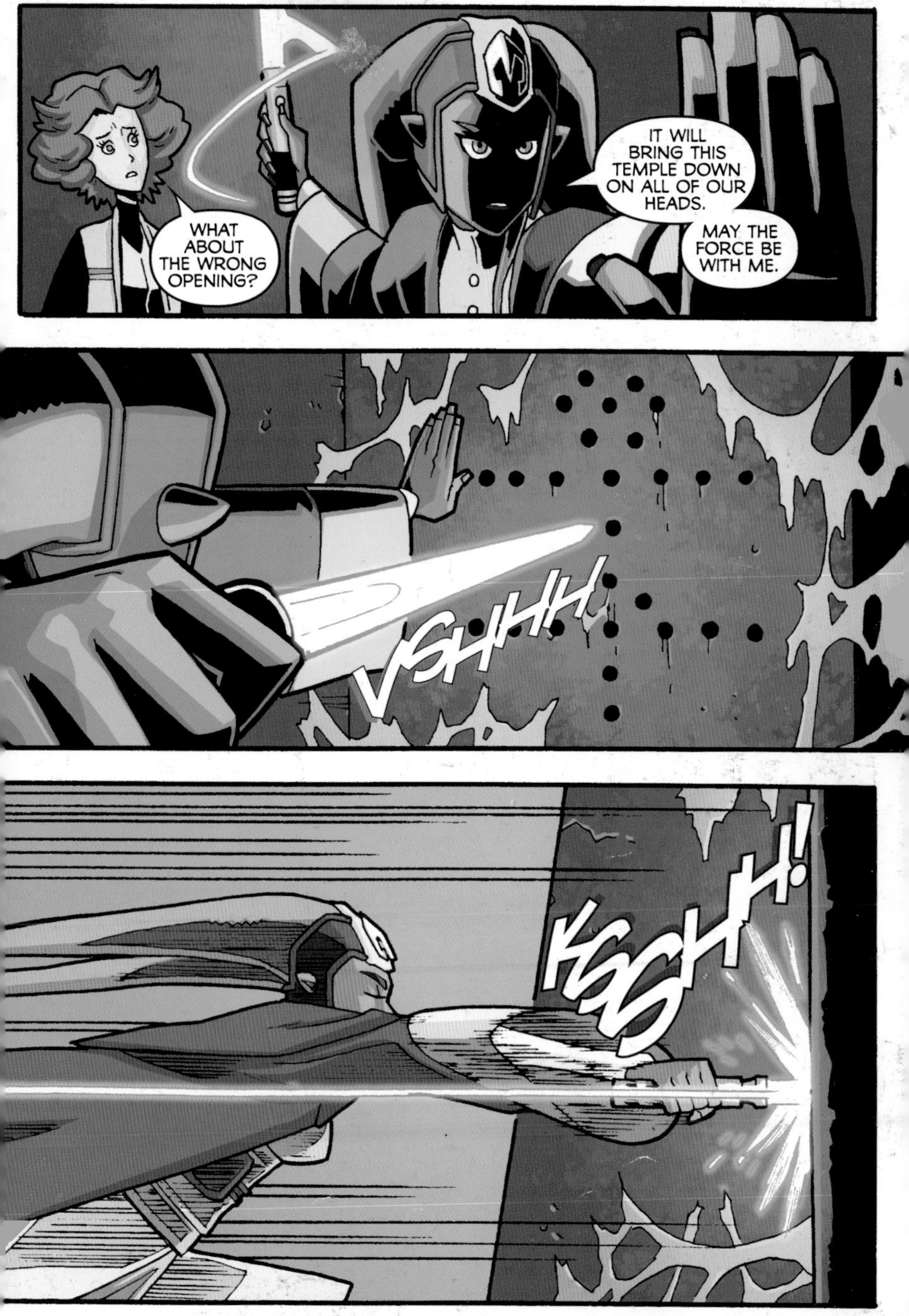
WHAT ABOUT THE WRONG OPENING?
IT WILL BRING THIS TEMPLE DOWN ON ALL OF OUR HEADS.
MAY THE FORCE BE WITH ME.
VSHHH!
KSSHH!

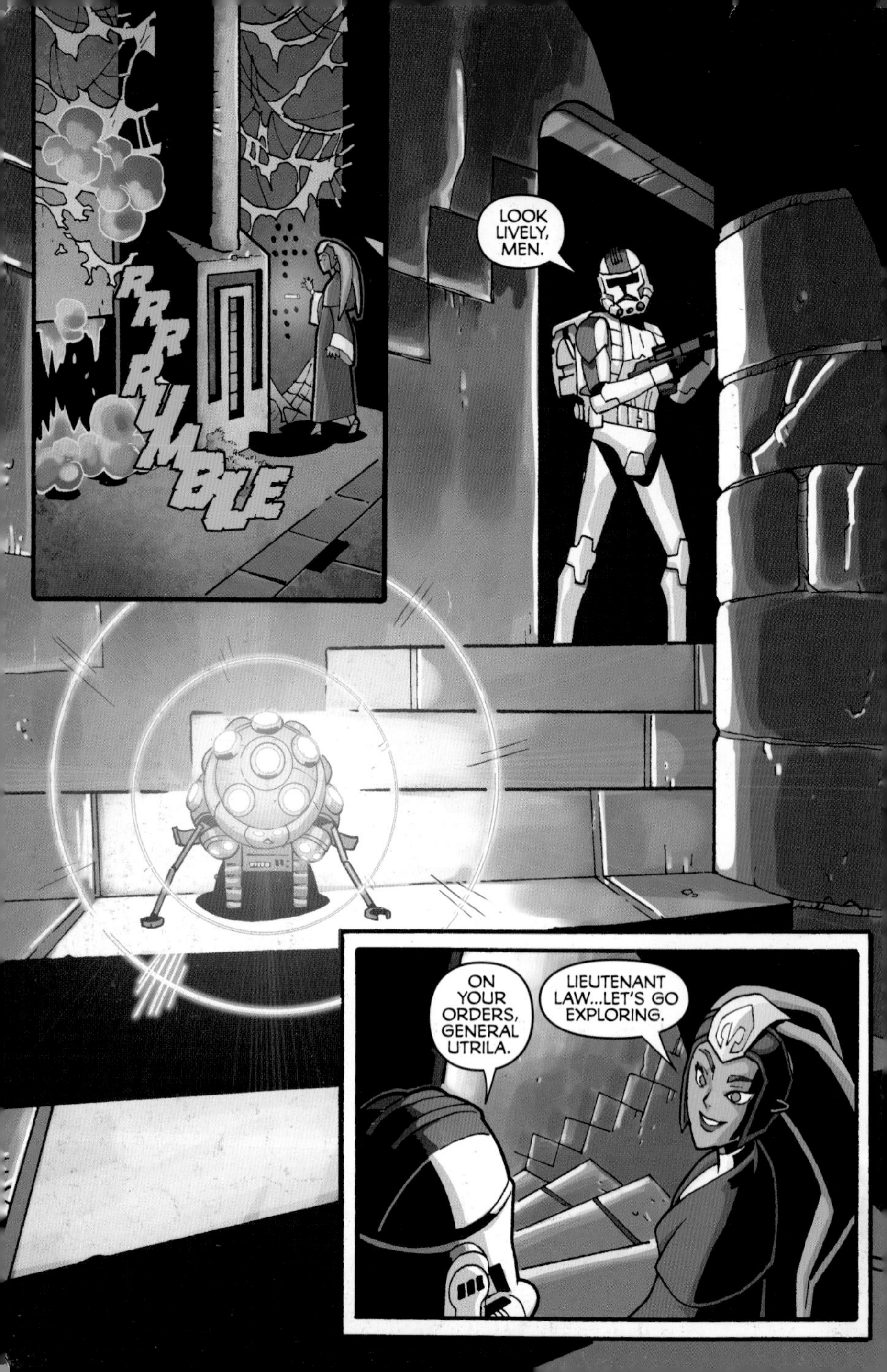
RRRRRUMBLE
LOOK LIVELY, MEN.
LIEUTENANT LAW...LET'S GO EXPLORING.
ON YOUR ORDERS, GENERAL UTRILA.

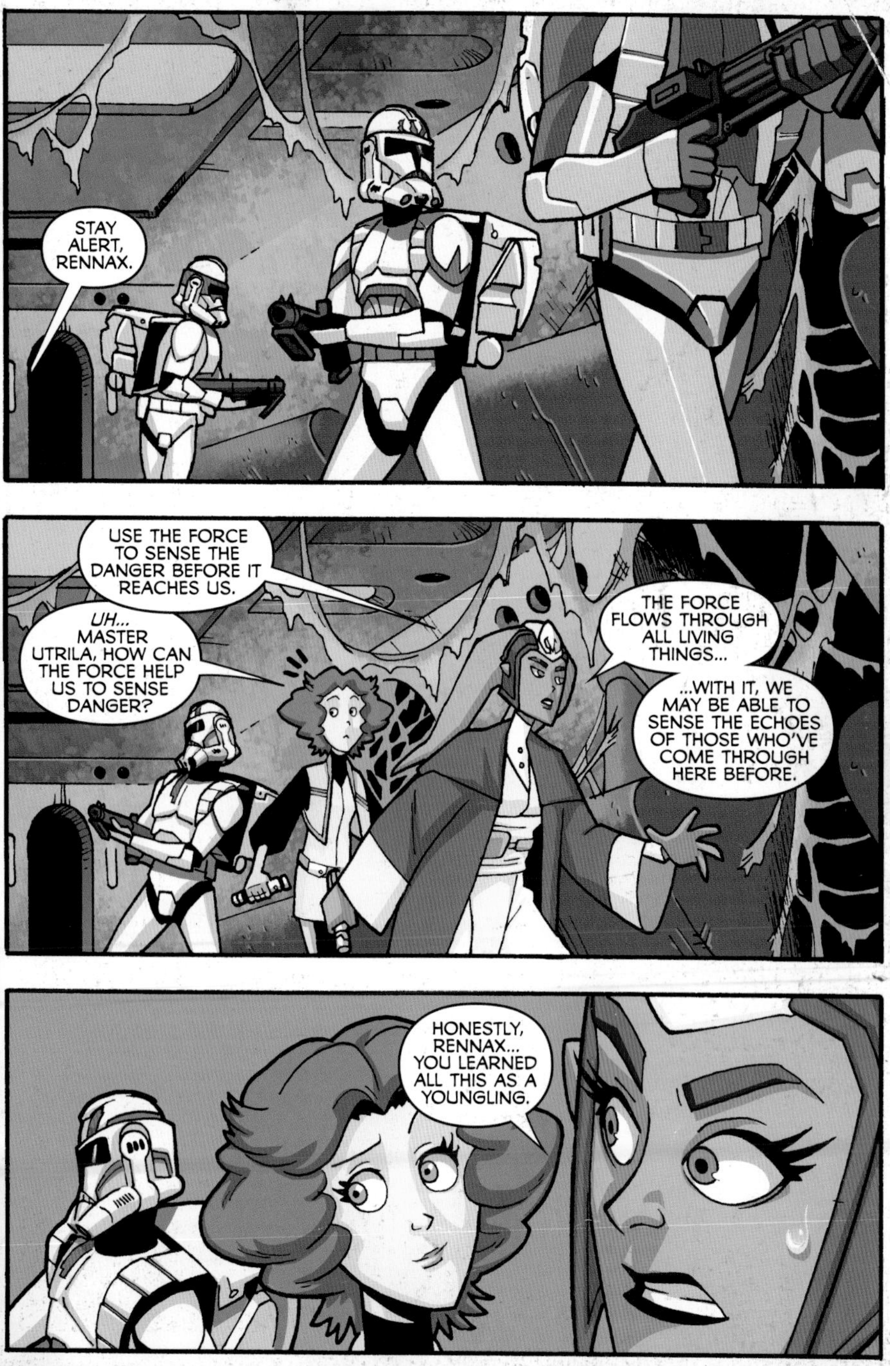
STAY ALERT, RENNAX.
USE THE FORCE TO SENSE THE DANGER BEFORE IT REACHES US.
UH... MASTER UTRILA, HOW CAN THE FORCE HELP US TO SENSE DANGER?
THE FORCE FLOWS THROUGH ALL LIVING THINGS...
...WITH IT, WE MAY BE ABLE TO SENSE THE ECHOES OF THOSE WHO'VE COME THROUGH HERE BEFORE.
HONESTLY, RENNAX... YOU LEARNED ALL THIS AS A YOUNGLING.

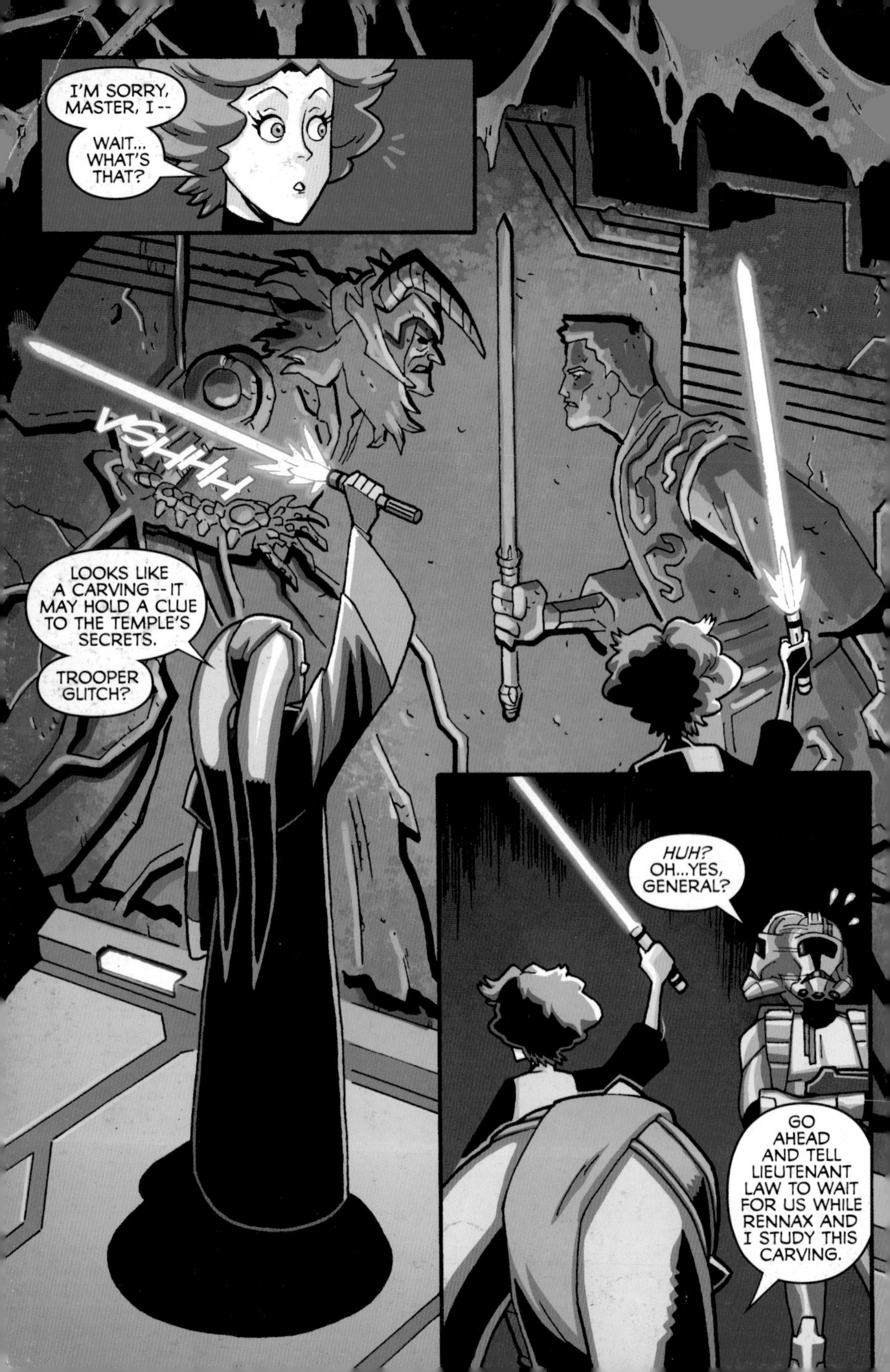
I'M SORRY, MASTER, I --
WAIT... WHAT'S THAT?
VSHHH
LOOKS LIKE A CARVING -- IT MAY HOLD A CLUE TO THE TEMPLE'S SECRETS.
TROOPER GLITCH?
HUH? OH...YES, GENERAL?
GO AHEAD AND TELL LIEUTENANT LAW TO WAIT FOR US WHILE RENNAX AND I STUDY THIS CARVING.

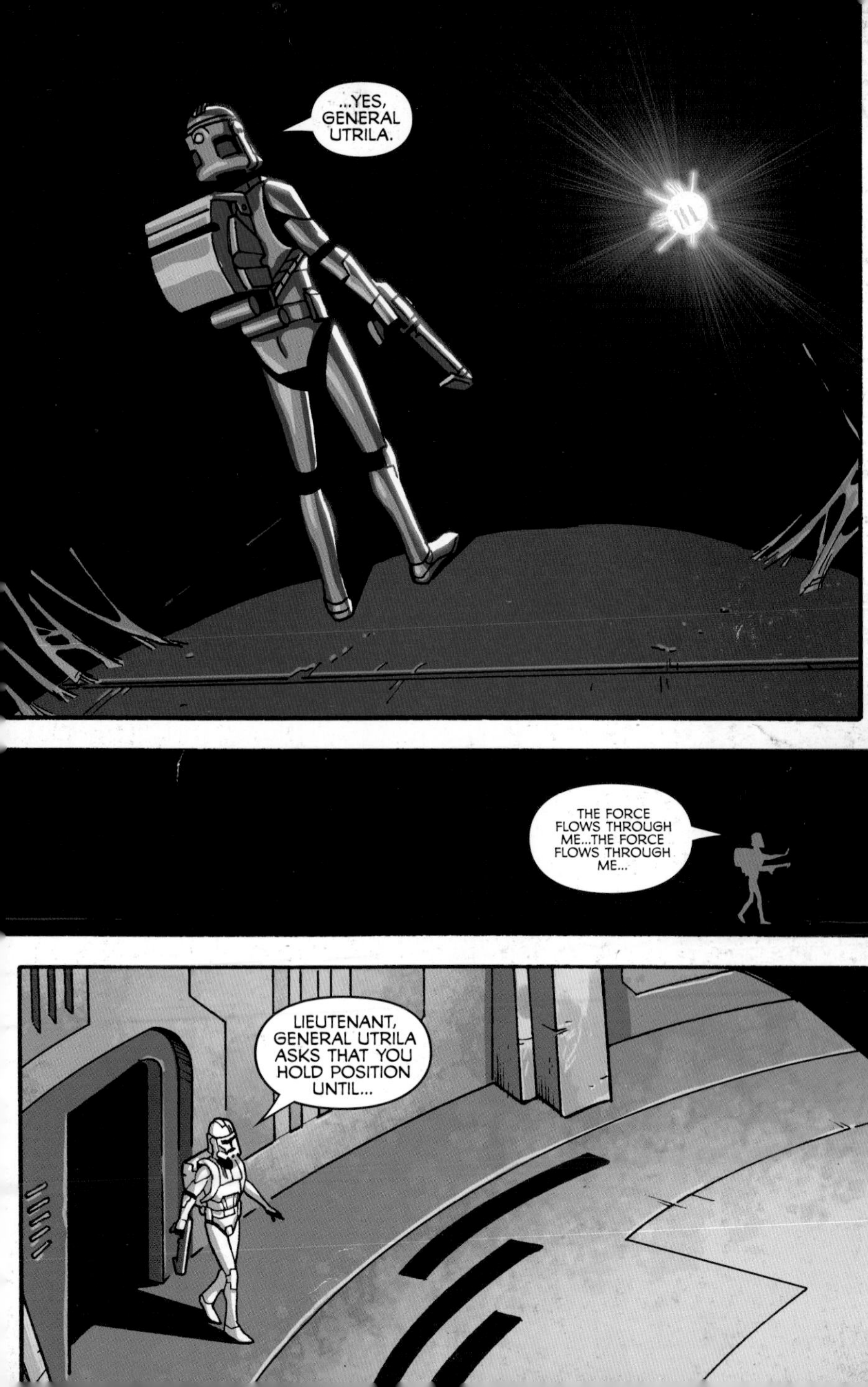
...YES, GENERAL UTRILA.
THE FORCE FLOWS THROUGH ME...THE FORCE FLOWS THROUGH ME...
LIEUTENANT, GENERAL UTRILA ASKS THAT YOU HOLD POSITION UNTIL...

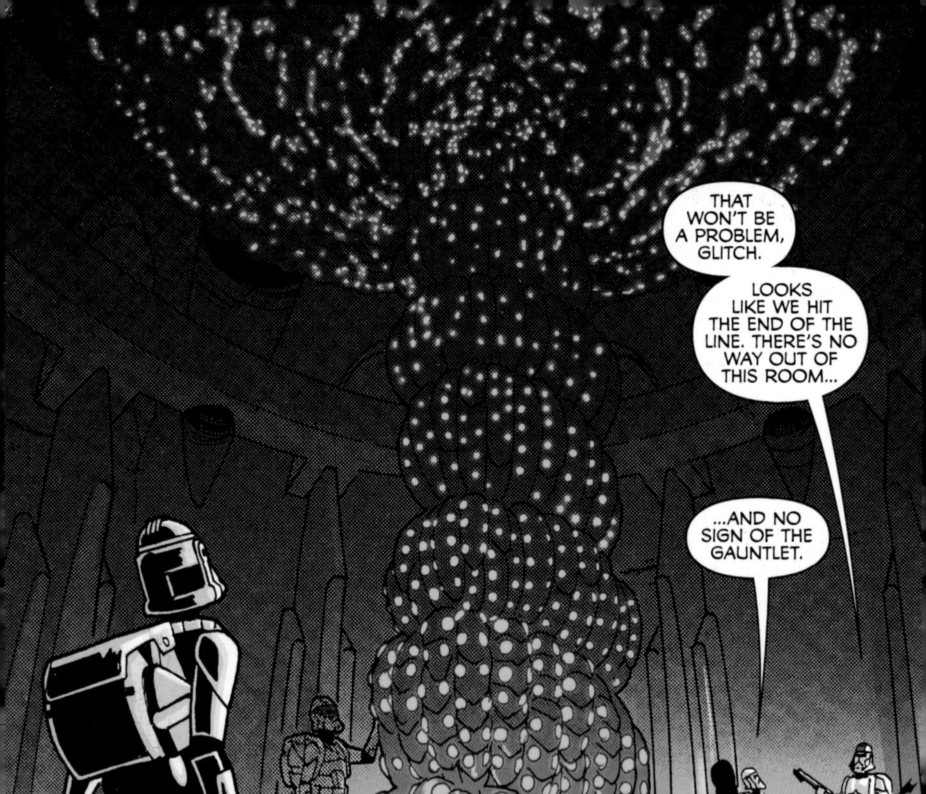
THAT WON'T BE A PROBLEM, GLITCH.
LOOKS LIKE WE HIT THE END OF THE LINE. THERE'S NO WAY OUT OF THIS ROOM...
...AND NO SIGN OF THE GAUNTLET.

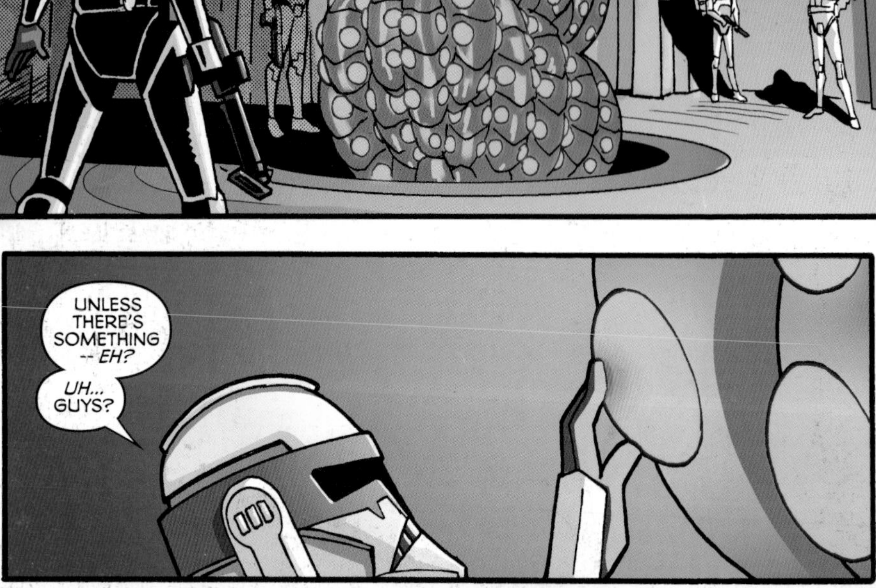
UNLESS THERE'S SOMETHING -- EH?
UH... GUYS?

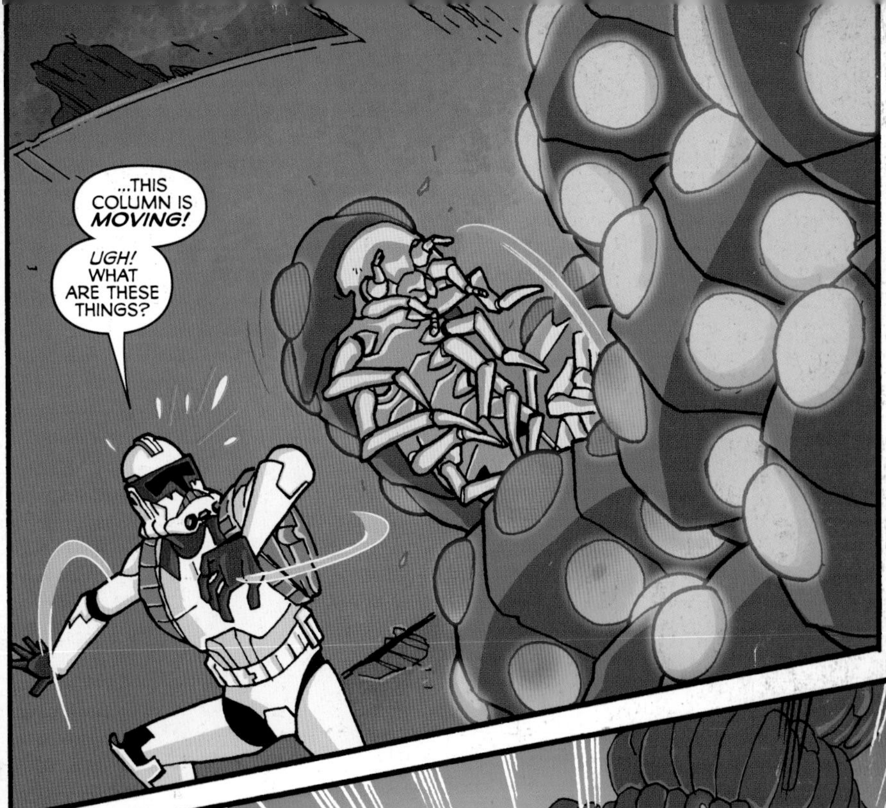
...THIS COLUMN IS *MOVING!*
UGH! WHAT ARE THESE THINGS?

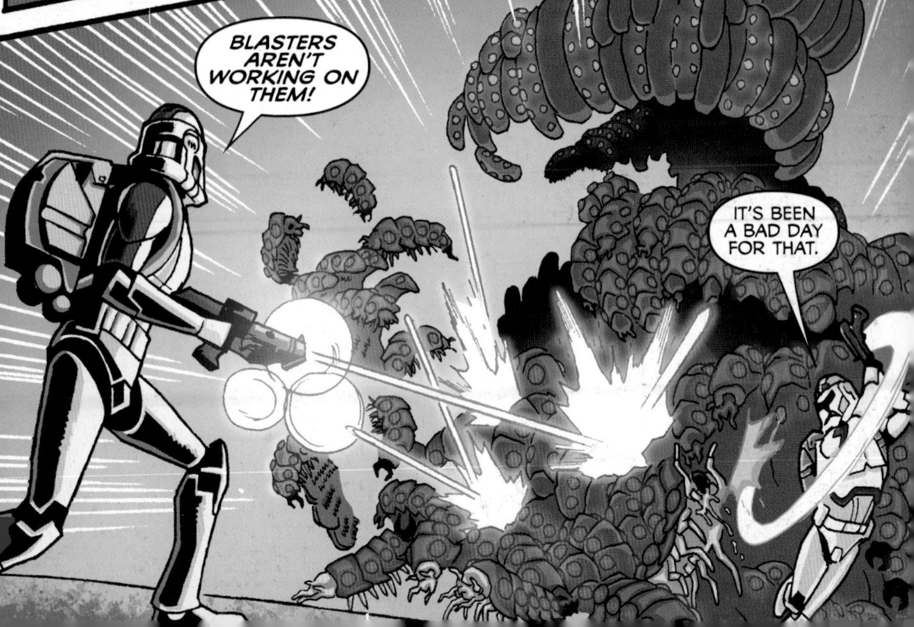
BLASTERS AREN'T WORKING ON THEM!
IT'S BEEN A BAD DAY FOR THAT.

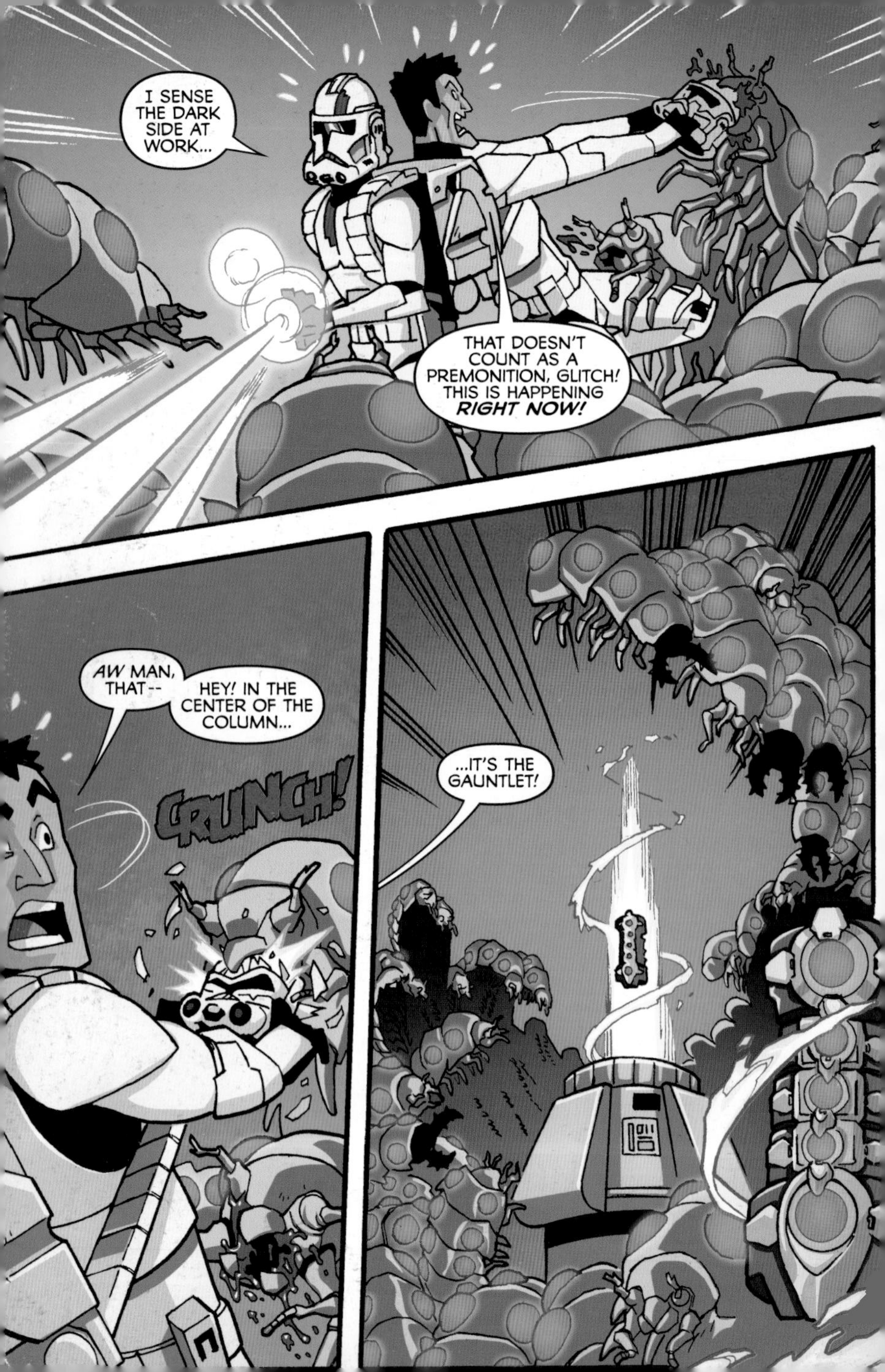
I SENSE THE DARK SIDE AT WORK...
THAT DOESN'T COUNT AS A PREMONITION, GLITCH! THIS IS HAPPENING *RIGHT NOW!*
AW MAN, THAT--
HEY! IN THE CENTER OF THE COLUMN...
CRUNCH!
...IT'S THE GAUNTLET!

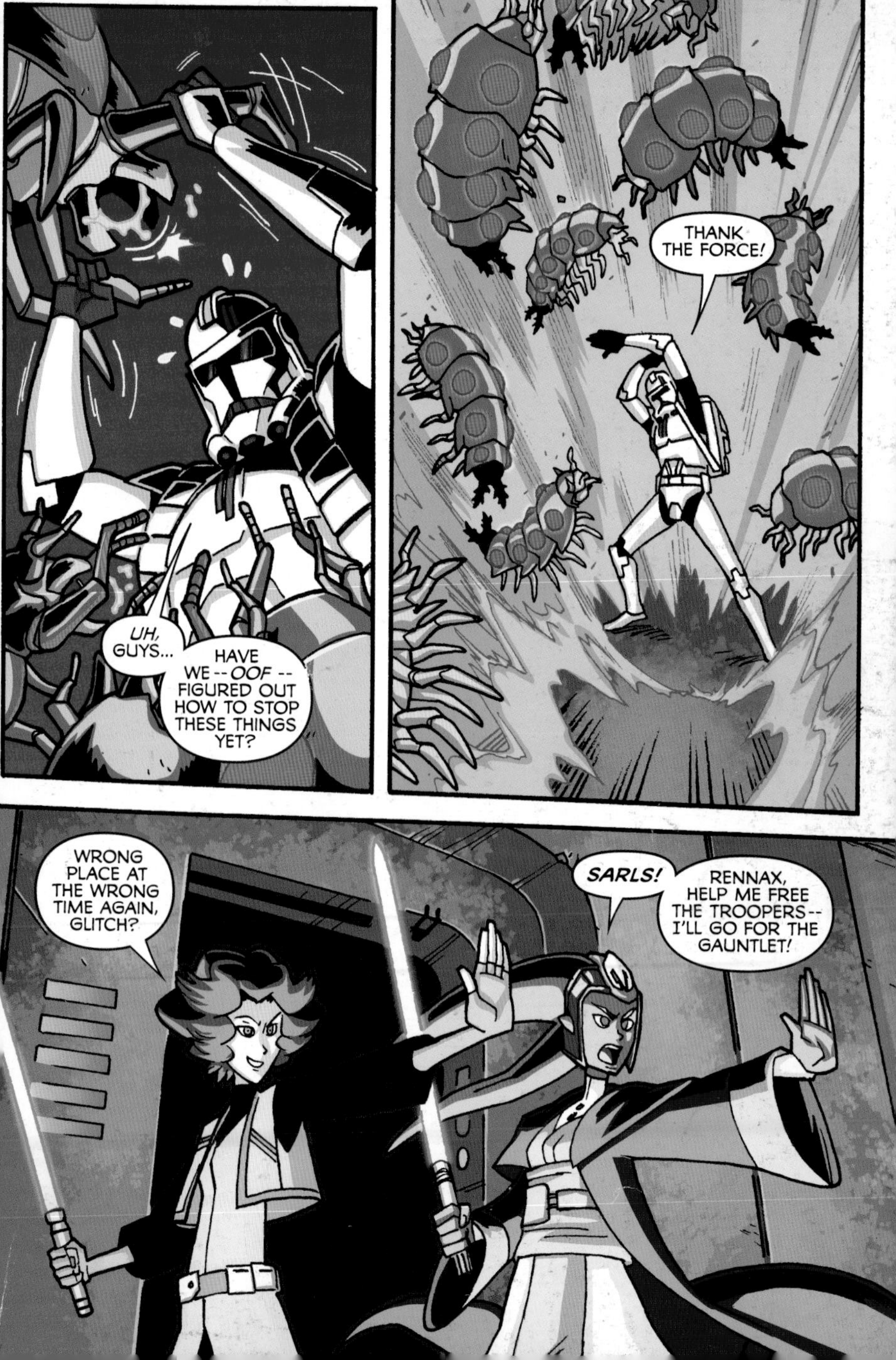
UH, GUYS...
HAVE WE -- OOF -- FIGURED OUT HOW TO STOP THESE THINGS YET?
THANK THE FORCE!
WRONG PLACE AT THE WRONG TIME AGAIN, GLITCH?
SARLS!
RENNAX, HELP ME FREE THE TROOPERS-- I'LL GO FOR THE GAUNTLET!

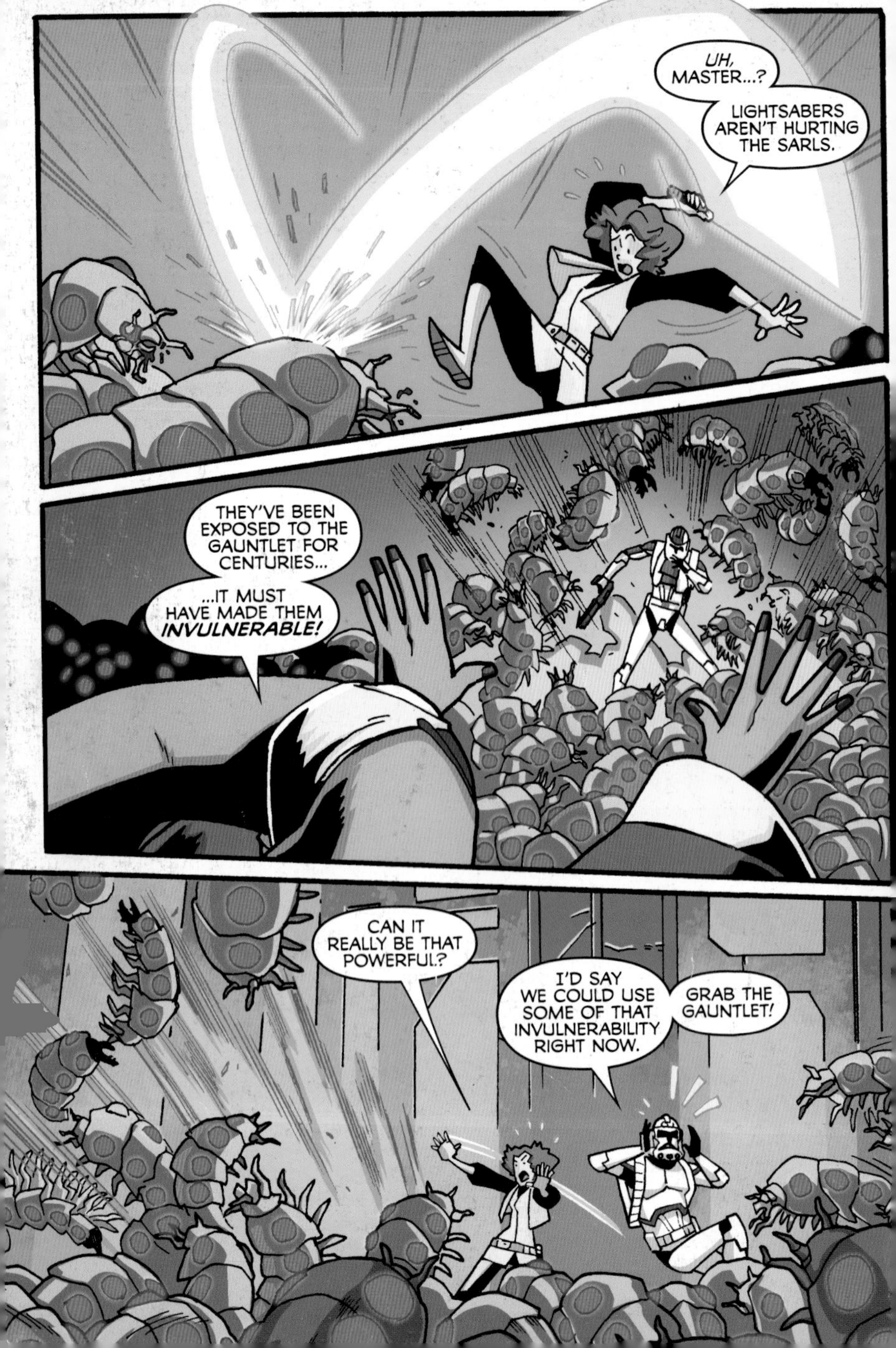
UH, MASTER...?
LIGHTSABERS AREN'T HURTING THE SARLS.
THEY'VE BEEN EXPOSED TO THE GAUNTLET FOR CENTURIES...
...IT MUST HAVE MADE THEM *INVULNERABLE!*
CAN IT REALLY BE THAT POWERFUL?
I'D SAY WE COULD USE SOME OF THAT INVULNERABILITY RIGHT NOW.
GRAB THE GAUNTLET!

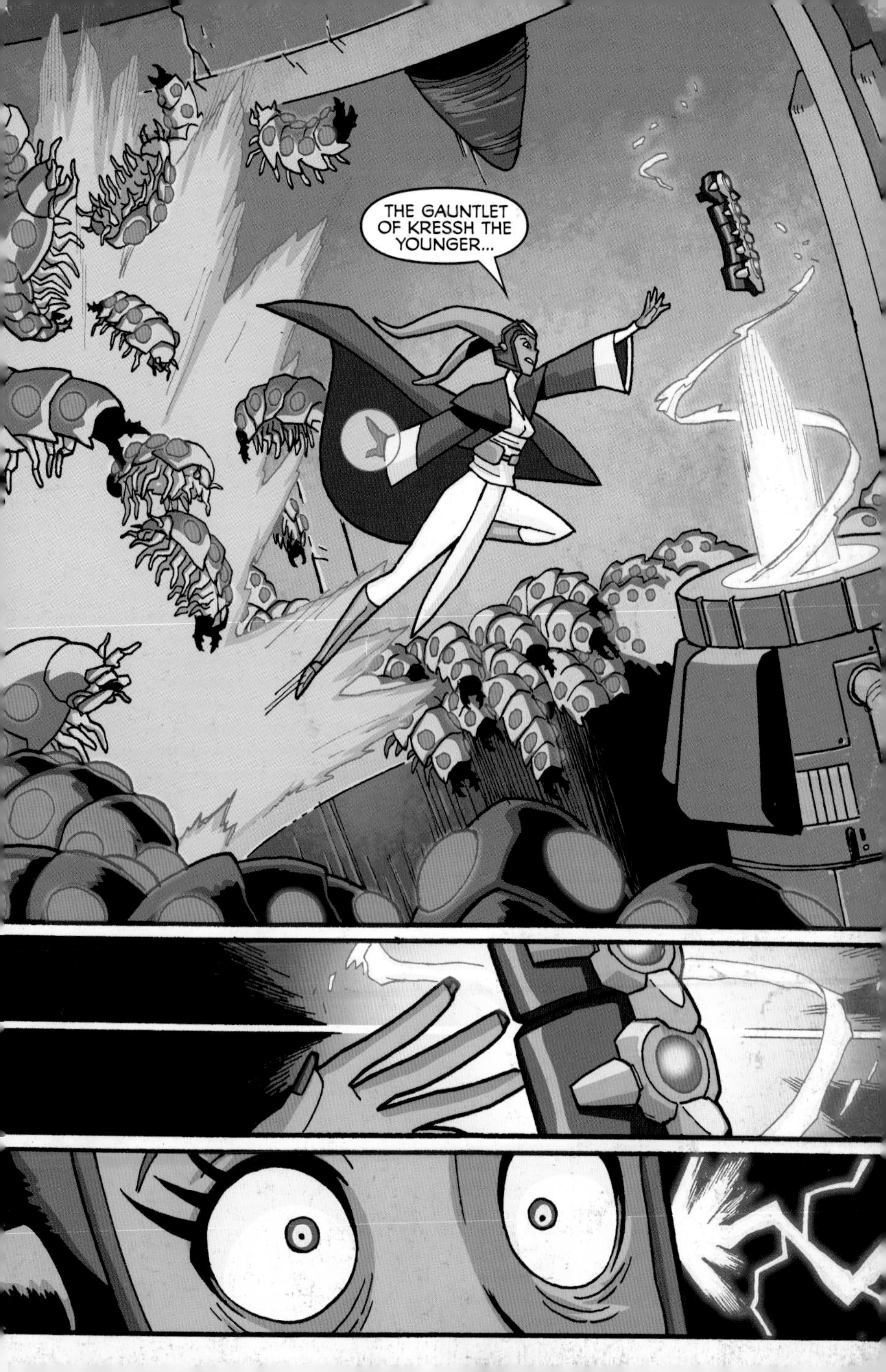
THE GAUNTLET OF KRESSH THE YOUNGER...

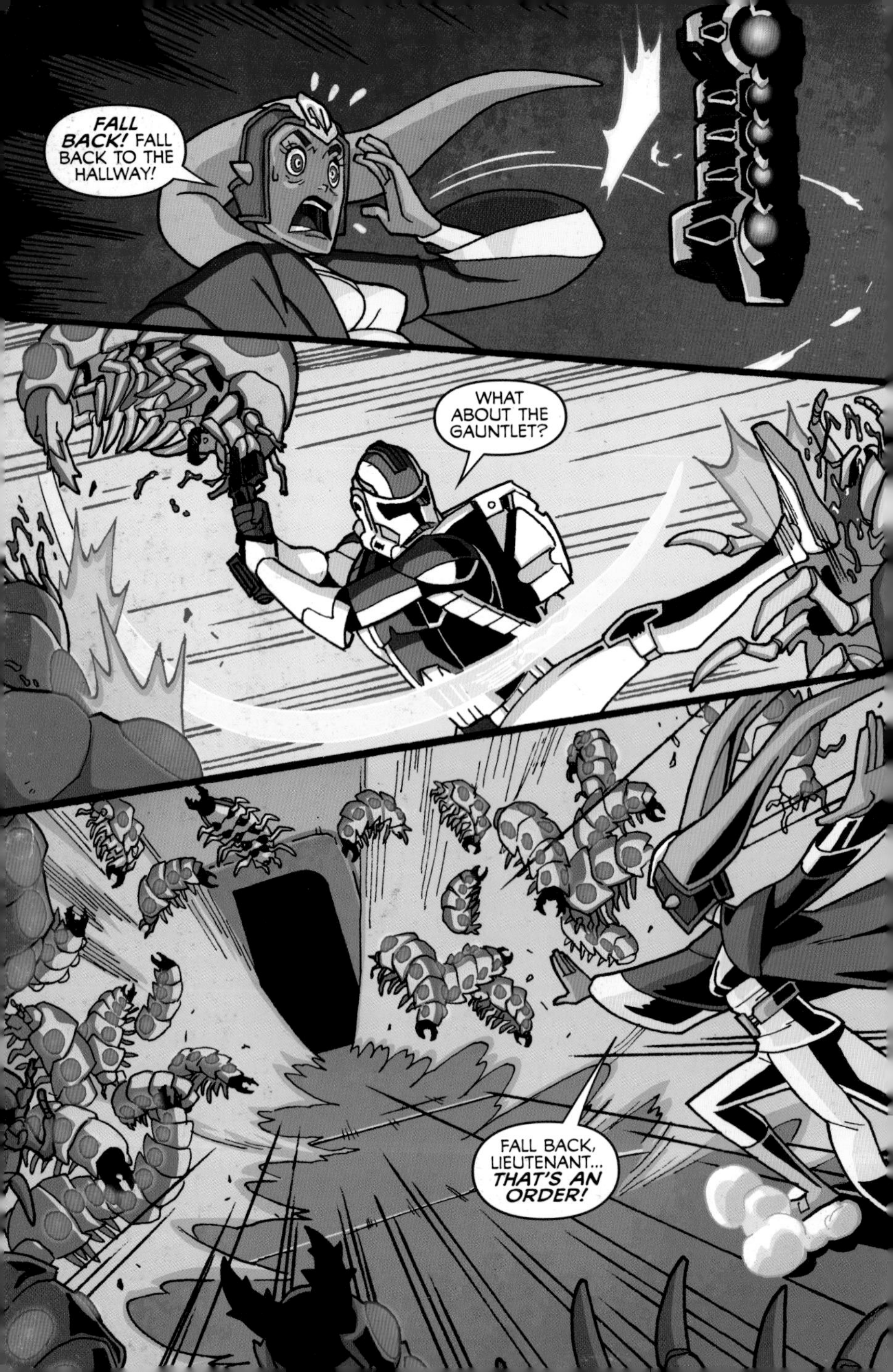
FALL BACK! FALL BACK TO THE HALLWAY!
WHAT ABOUT THE GAUNTLET?
FALL BACK, LIEUTENANT... THAT'S AN ORDER!

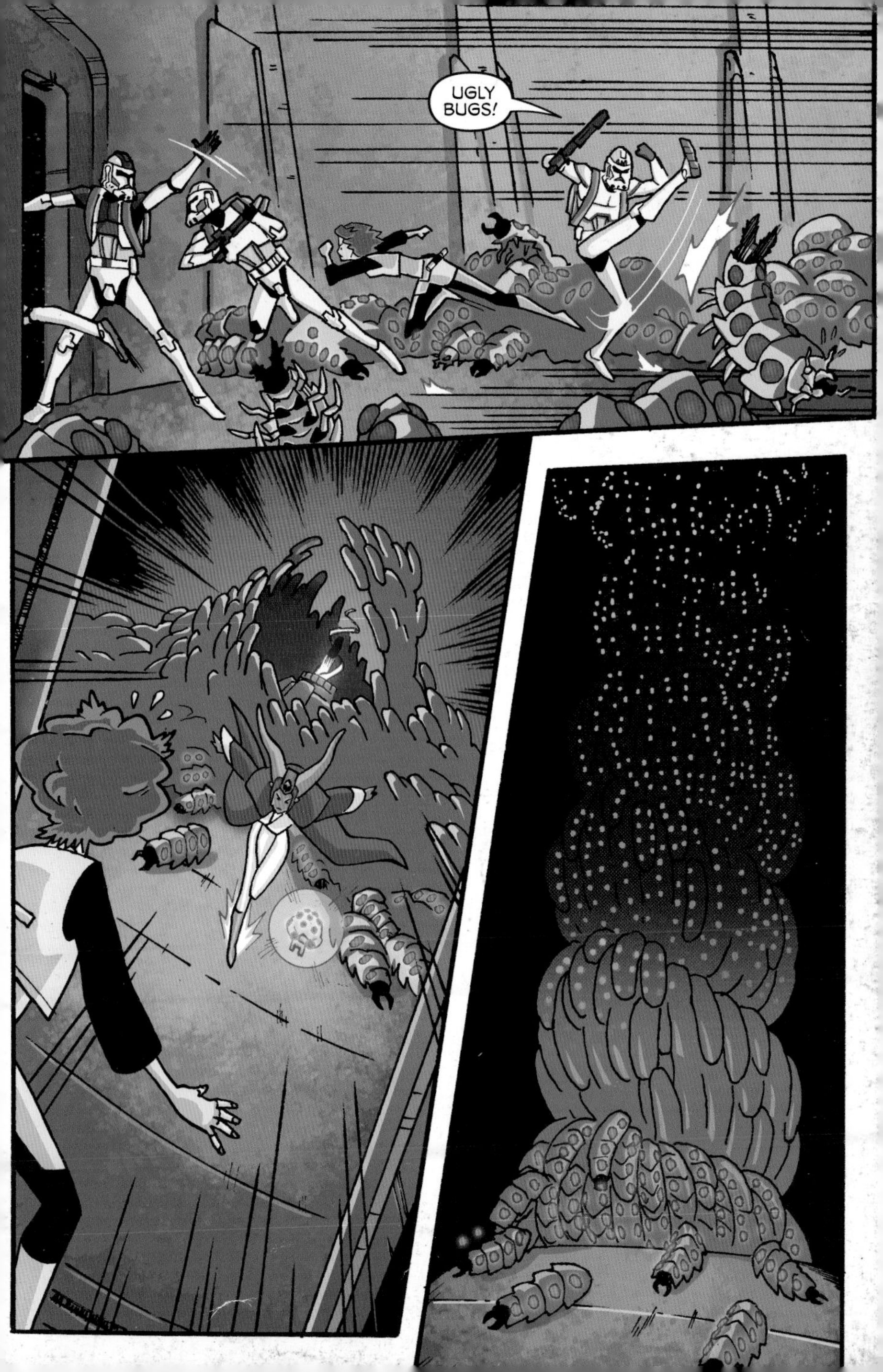
UGLY BUGS!

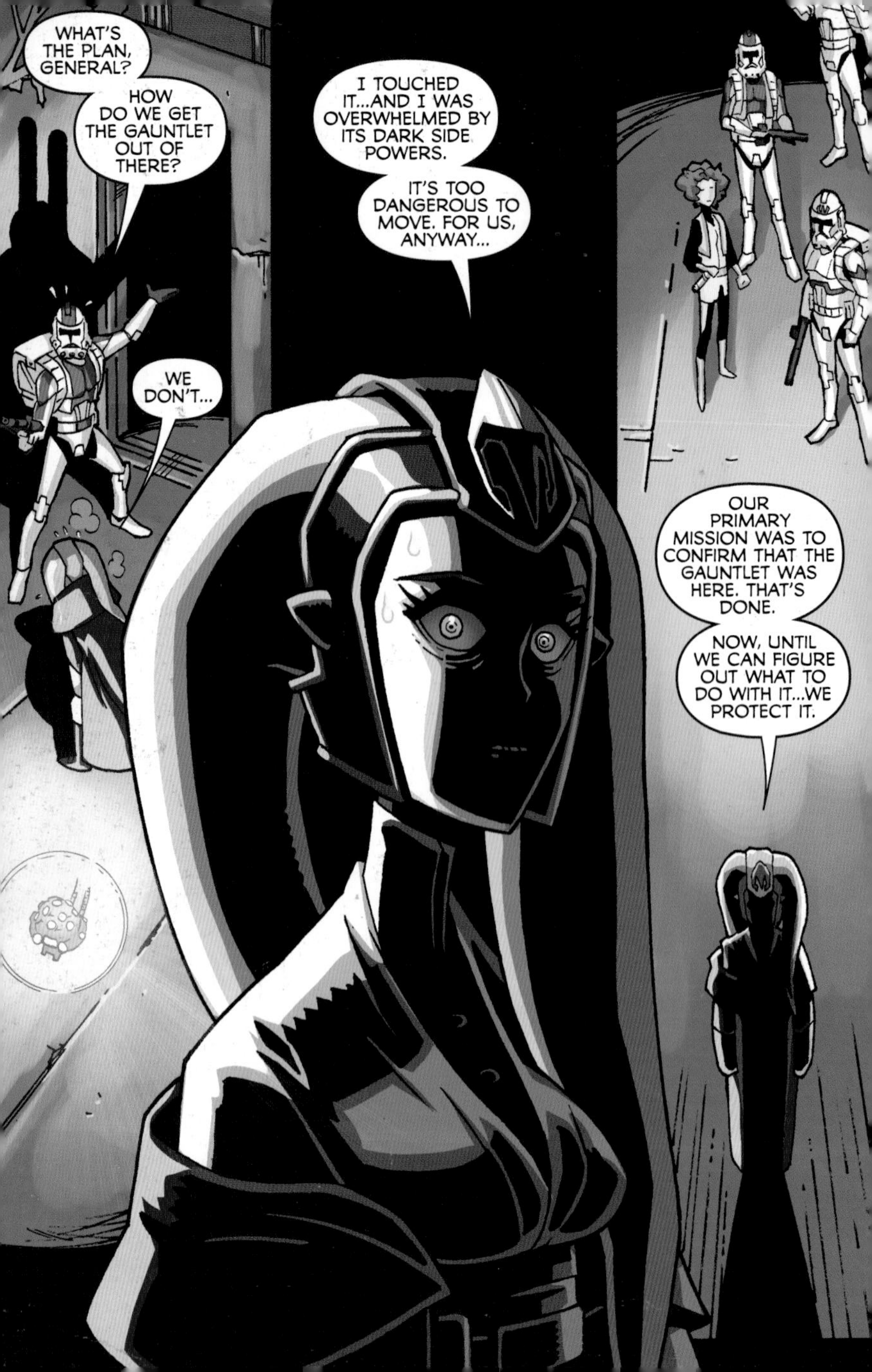
WHAT'S THE PLAN, GENERAL?
HOW DO WE GET THE GAUNTLET OUT OF THERE?
WE DON'T...
I TOUCHED IT...AND I WAS OVERWHELMED BY ITS DARK SIDE POWERS.
IT'S TOO DANGEROUS TO MOVE. FOR US, ANYWAY...
OUR PRIMARY MISSION WAS TO CONFIRM THAT THE GAUNTLET WAS HERE. THAT'S DONE.
NOW, UNTIL WE CAN FIGURE OUT WHAT TO DO WITH IT...WE PROTECT IT.

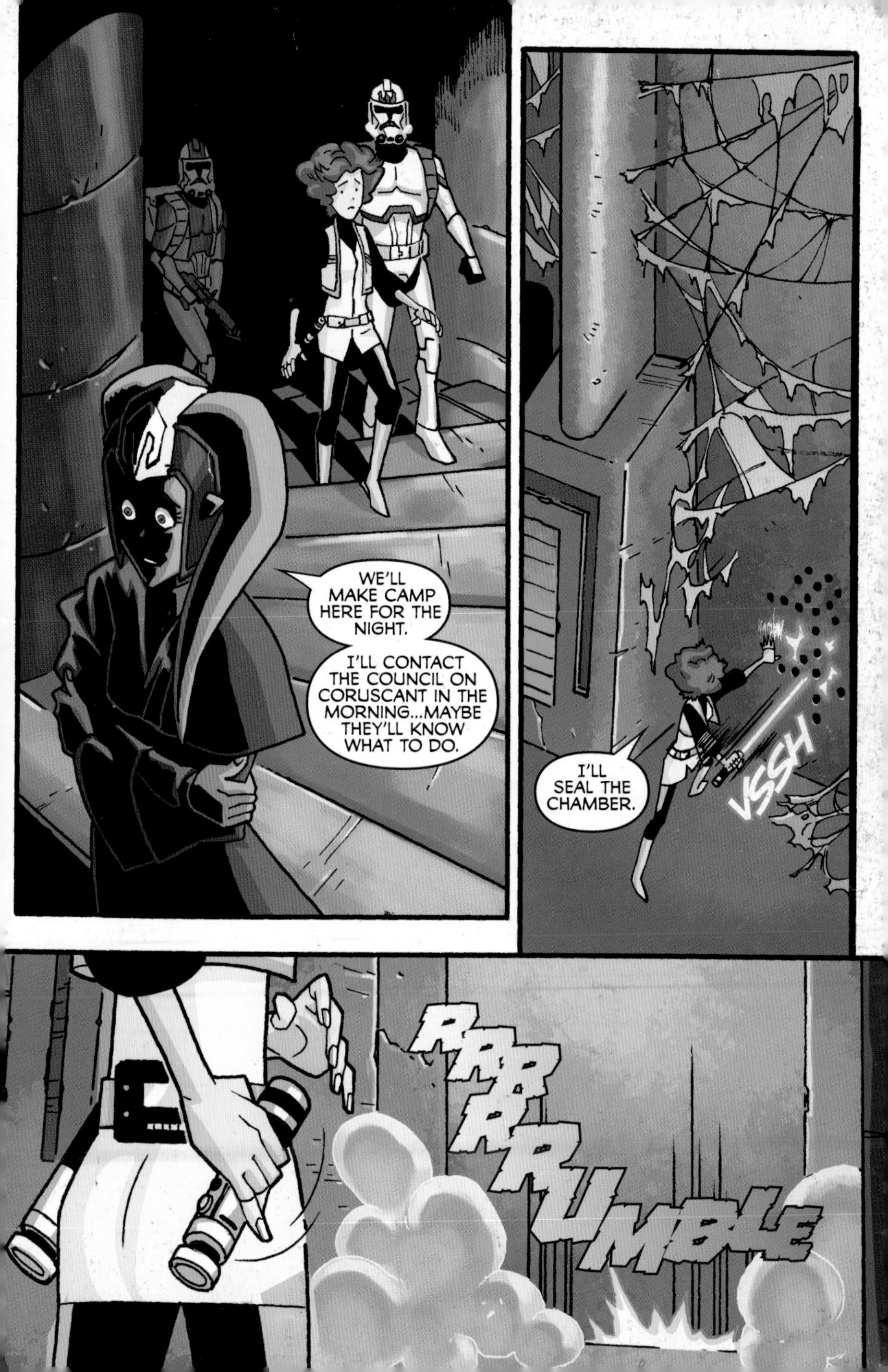
WE'LL MAKE CAMP HERE FOR THE NIGHT.
I'LL CONTACT THE COUNCIL ON CORUSCANT IN THE MORNING...MAYBE THEY'LL KNOW WHAT TO DO.
I'LL SEAL THE CHAMBER.
VSSH
RRRRRUMBLE

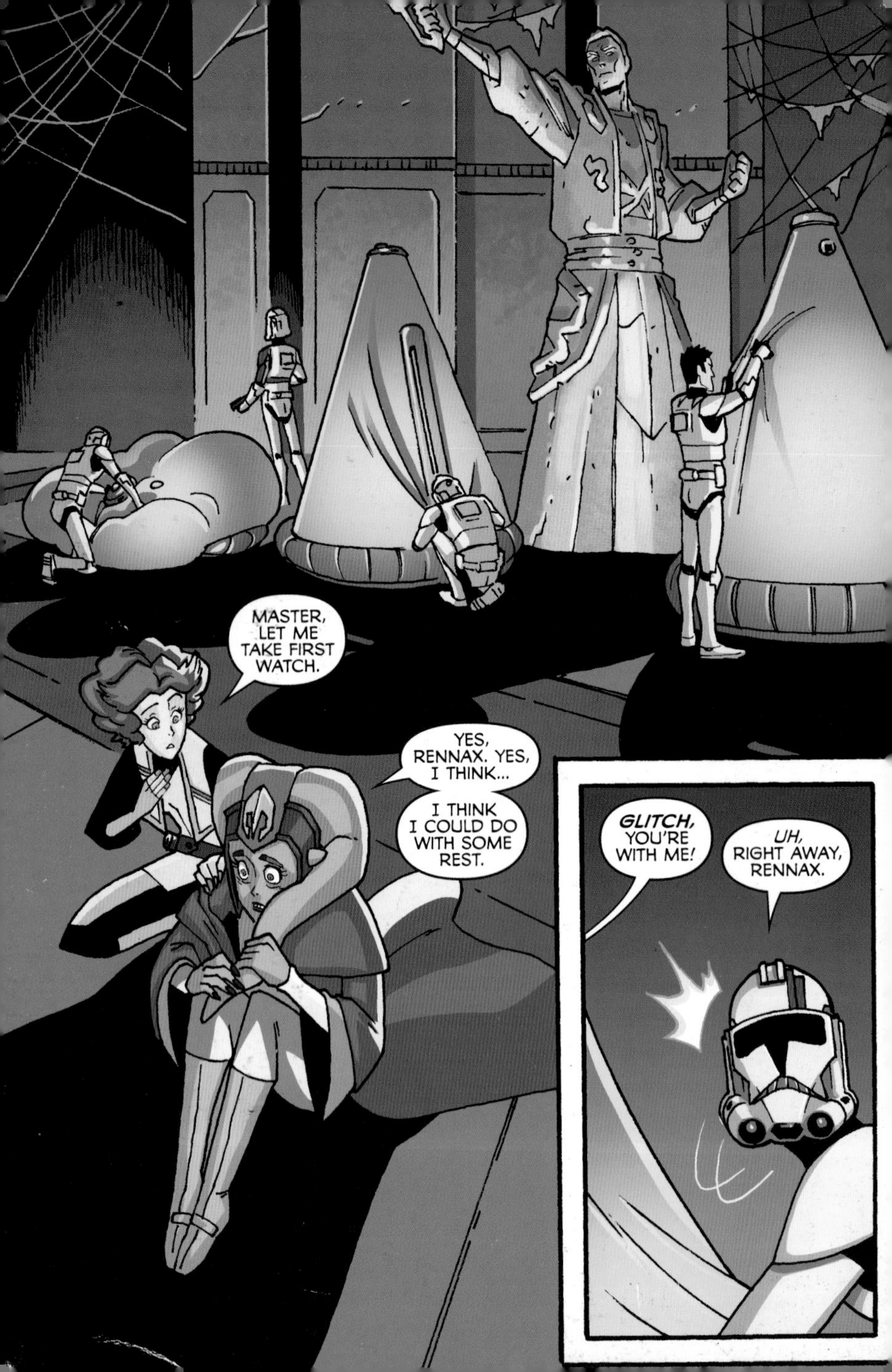
MASTER, LET ME TAKE FIRST WATCH.
YES, RENNAX. YES, I THINK...
I THINK I COULD DO WITH SOME REST.
GLITCH, YOU'RE WITH ME!
UH, RIGHT AWAY, RENNAX.

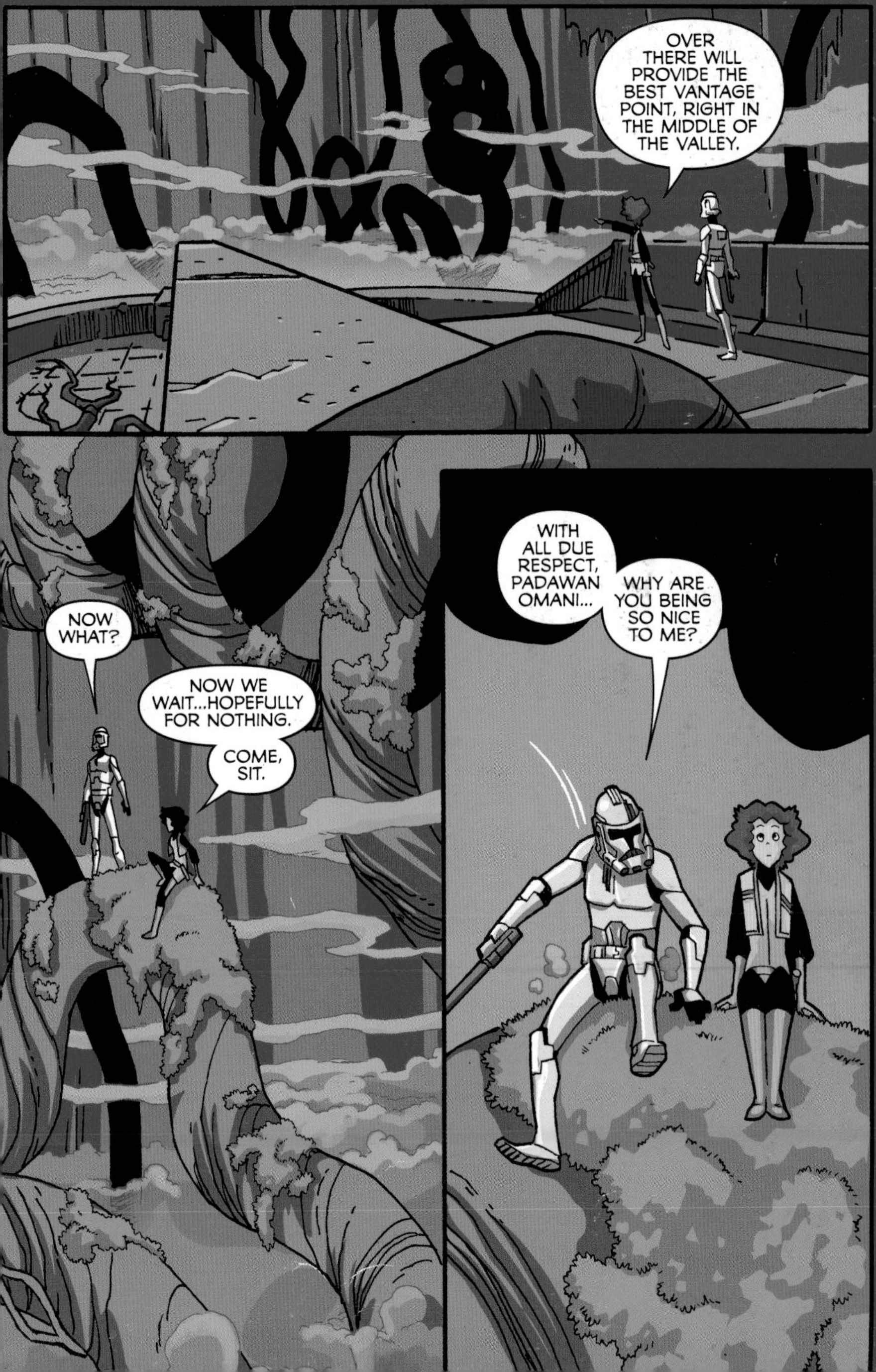
OVER THERE WILL PROVIDE THE BEST VANTAGE POINT, RIGHT IN THE MIDDLE OF THE VALLEY.
NOW WHAT?
NOW WE WAIT...HOPEFULLY FOR NOTHING.
COME, SIT.
WITH ALL DUE RESPECT, PADAWAN OMANI...
WHY ARE YOU BEING SO NICE TO ME?

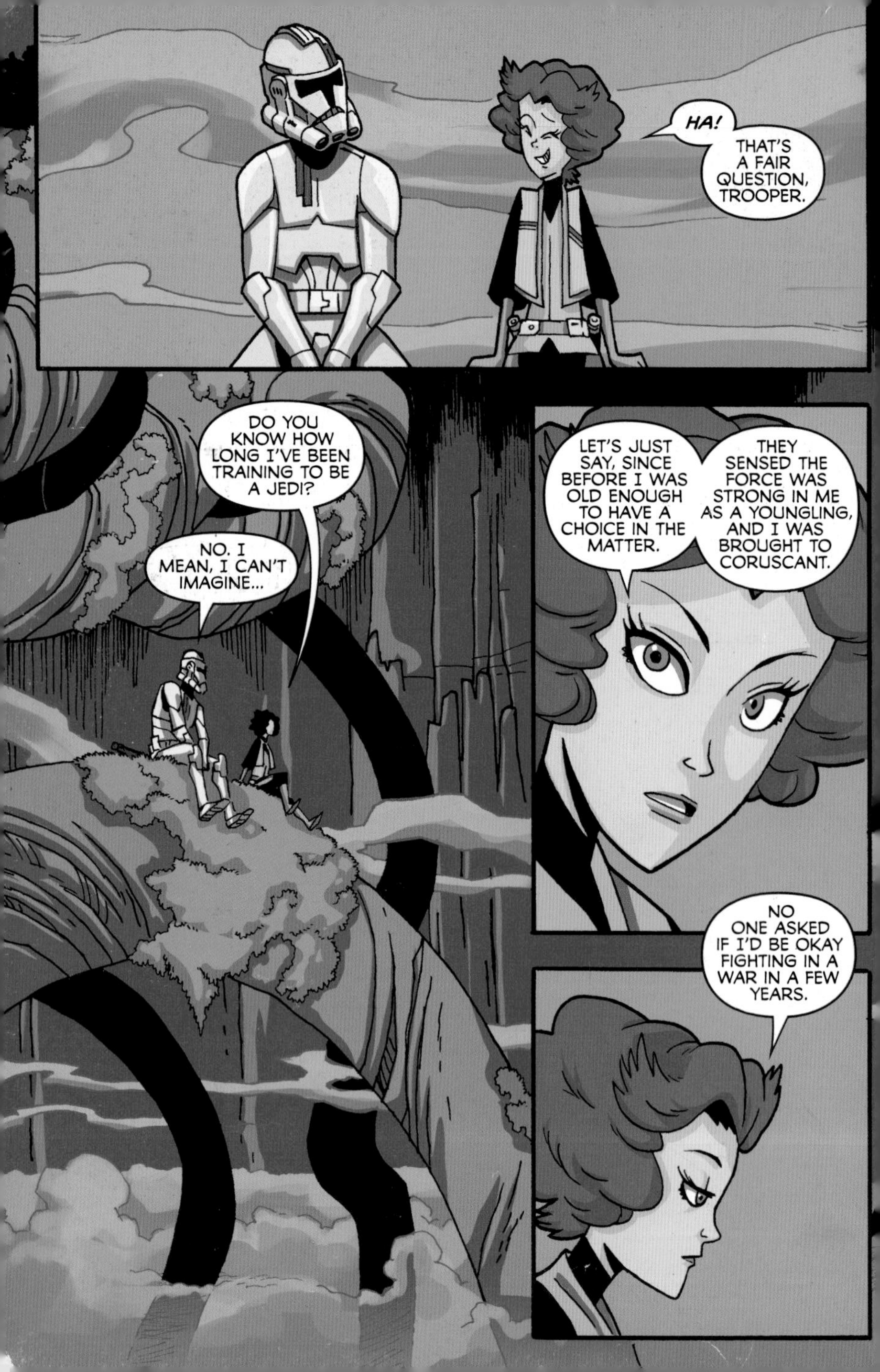
HA! THAT'S A FAIR QUESTION, TROOPER.
DO YOU KNOW HOW LONG I'VE BEEN TRAINING TO BE A JEDI?
NO. I MEAN, I CAN'T IMAGINE...
LET'S JUST SAY, SINCE BEFORE I WAS OLD ENOUGH TO HAVE A CHOICE IN THE MATTER.
THEY SENSED THE FORCE WAS STRONG IN ME AS A YOUNGLING, AND I WAS BROUGHT TO CORUSCANT.
NO ONE ASKED IF I'D BE OKAY FIGHTING IN A WAR IN A FEW YEARS.

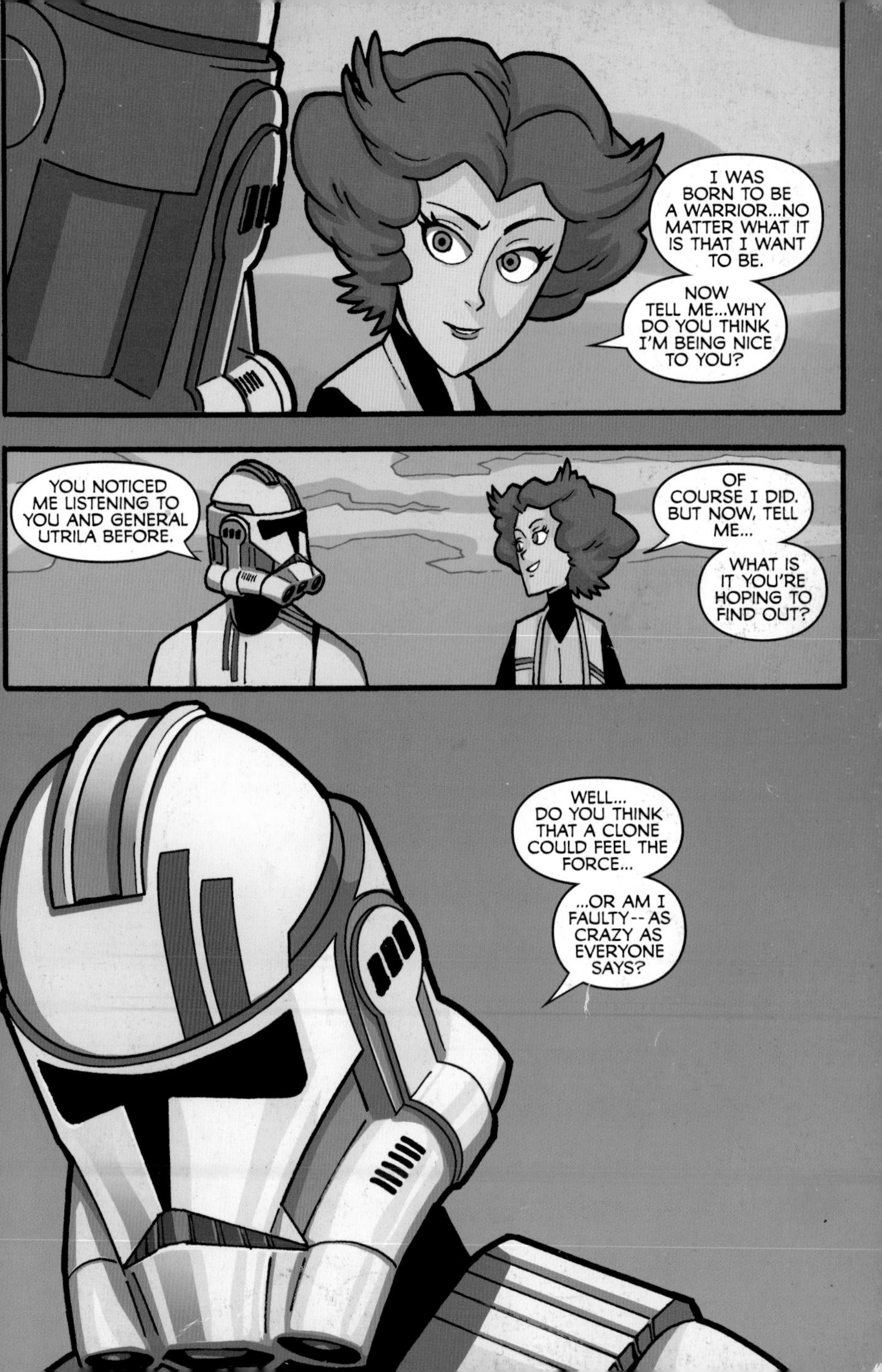
I WAS BORN TO BE A WARRIOR...NO MATTER WHAT IT IS THAT I WANT TO BE.
NOW TELL ME...WHY DO YOU THINK I'M BEING NICE TO YOU?
YOU NOTICED ME LISTENING TO YOU AND GENERAL UTRILA BEFORE.
OF COURSE I DID. BUT NOW, TELL ME...
WHAT IS IT YOU'RE HOPING TO FIND OUT?
WELL... DO YOU THINK THAT A CLONE COULD FEEL THE FORCE...
...OR AM I FAULTY-- AS CRAZY AS EVERYONE SAYS?

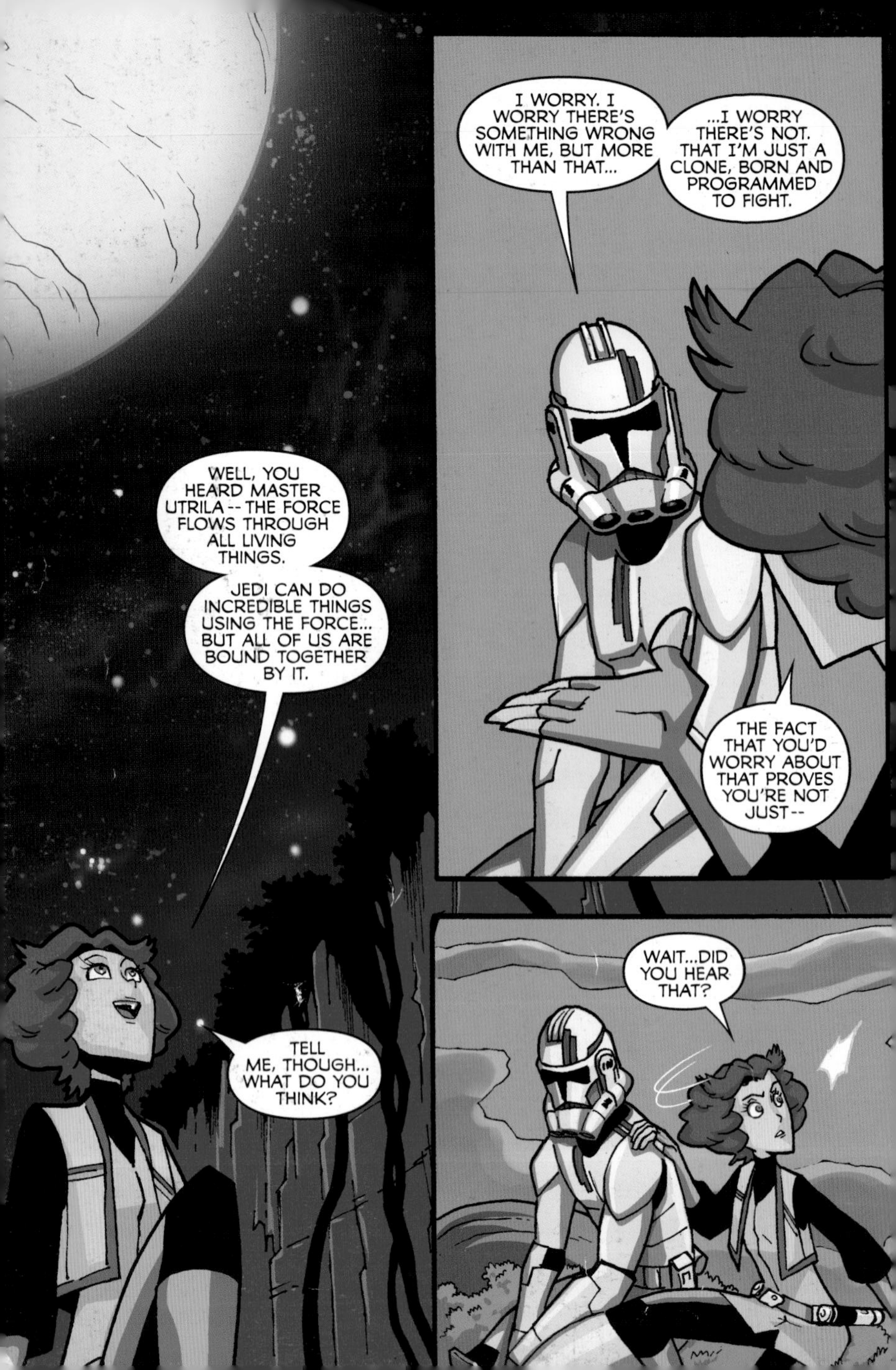
WELL, YOU HEARD MASTER UTRILA -- THE FORCE FLOWS THROUGH ALL LIVING THINGS.
JEDI CAN DO INCREDIBLE THINGS USING THE FORCE... BUT ALL OF US ARE BOUND TOGETHER BY IT.
TELL ME, THOUGH... WHAT DO YOU THINK?
I WORRY. I WORRY THERE'S SOMETHING WRONG WITH ME, BUT MORE THAN THAT...
...I WORRY THERE'S NOT. THAT I'M JUST A CLONE, BORN AND PROGRAMMED TO FIGHT.
THE FACT THAT YOU'D WORRY ABOUT THAT PROVES YOU'RE NOT JUST--
WAIT...DID YOU HEAR THAT?

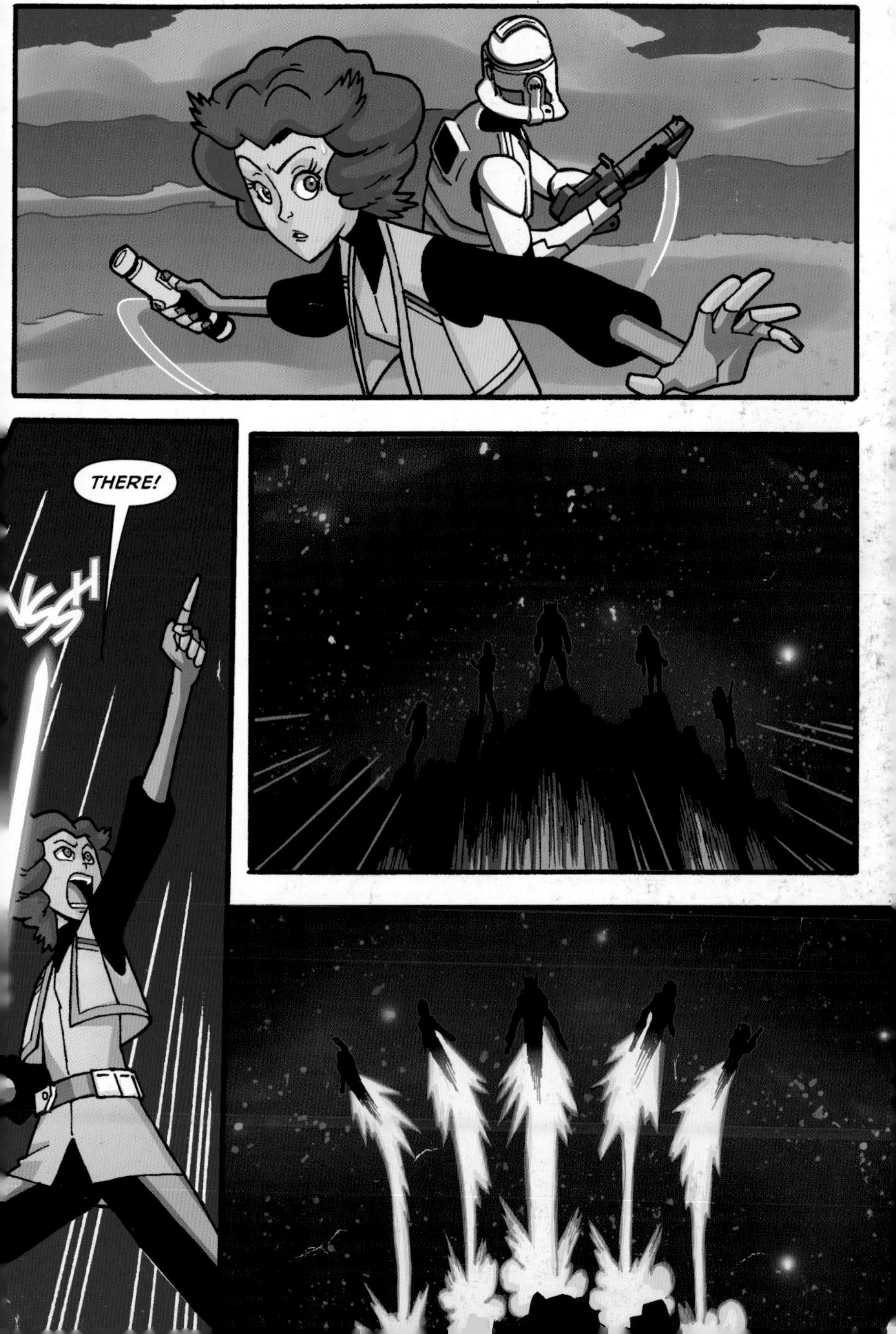
THERE!
VSSH

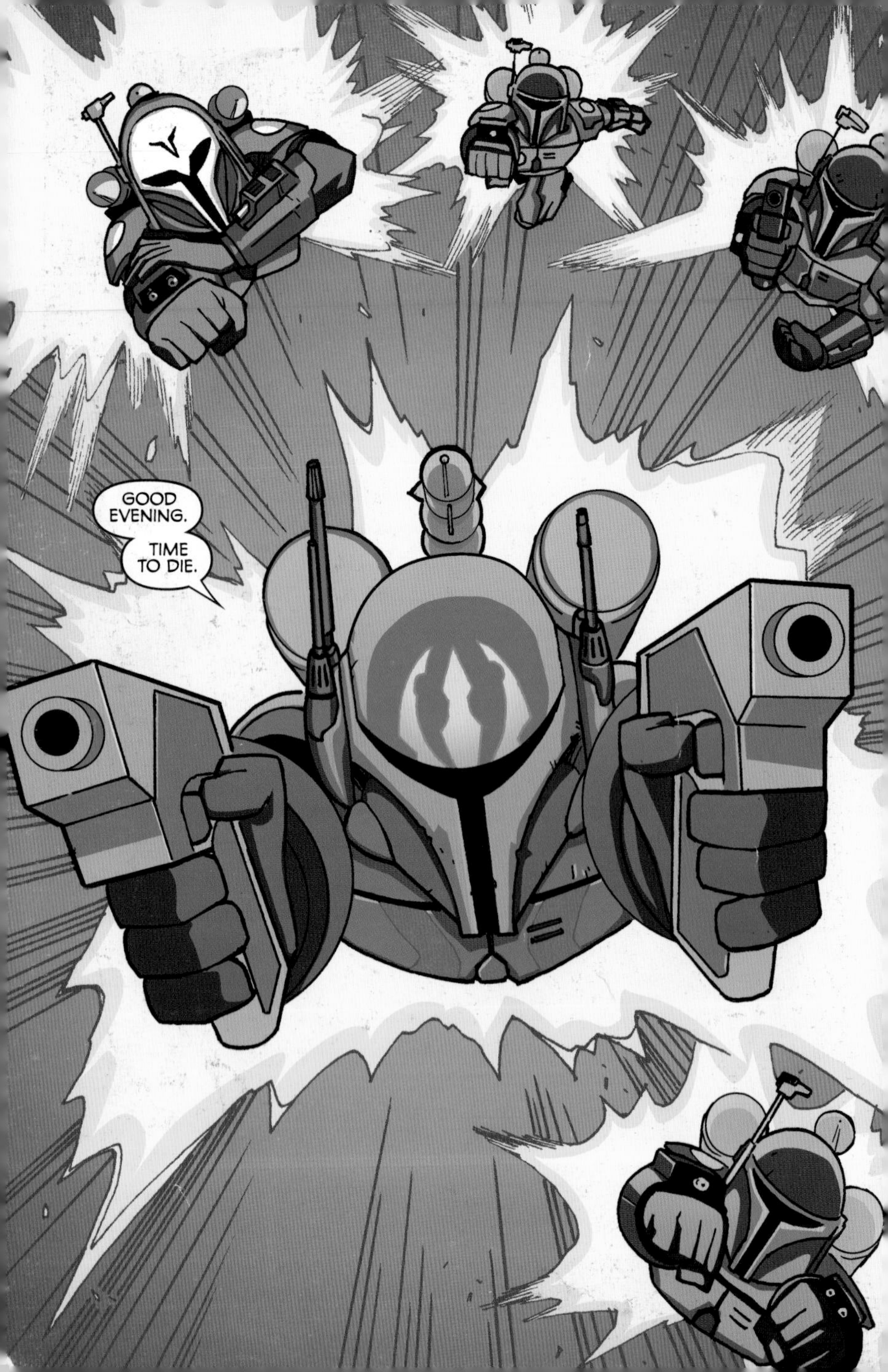
GOOD EVENING.
TIME TO DIE.

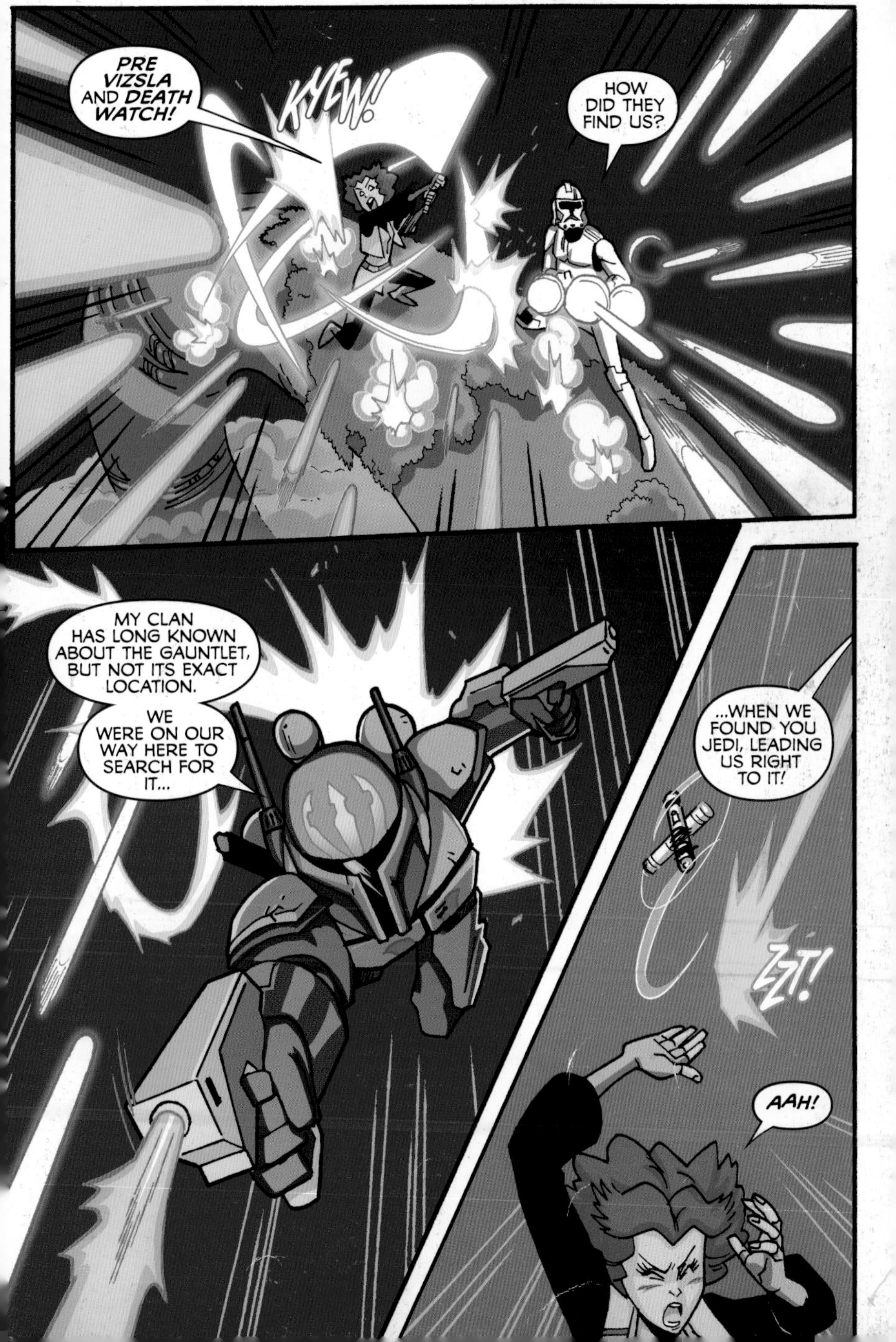
PRE VIZSLA AND DEATH WATCH!
KYEW!!
HOW DID THEY FIND US?
MY CLAN HAS LONG KNOWN ABOUT THE GAUNTLET, BUT NOT ITS EXACT LOCATION.
WE WERE ON OUR WAY HERE TO SEARCH FOR IT...
...WHEN WE FOUND YOU JEDI, LEADING US RIGHT TO IT!
ZZT!
AAH!

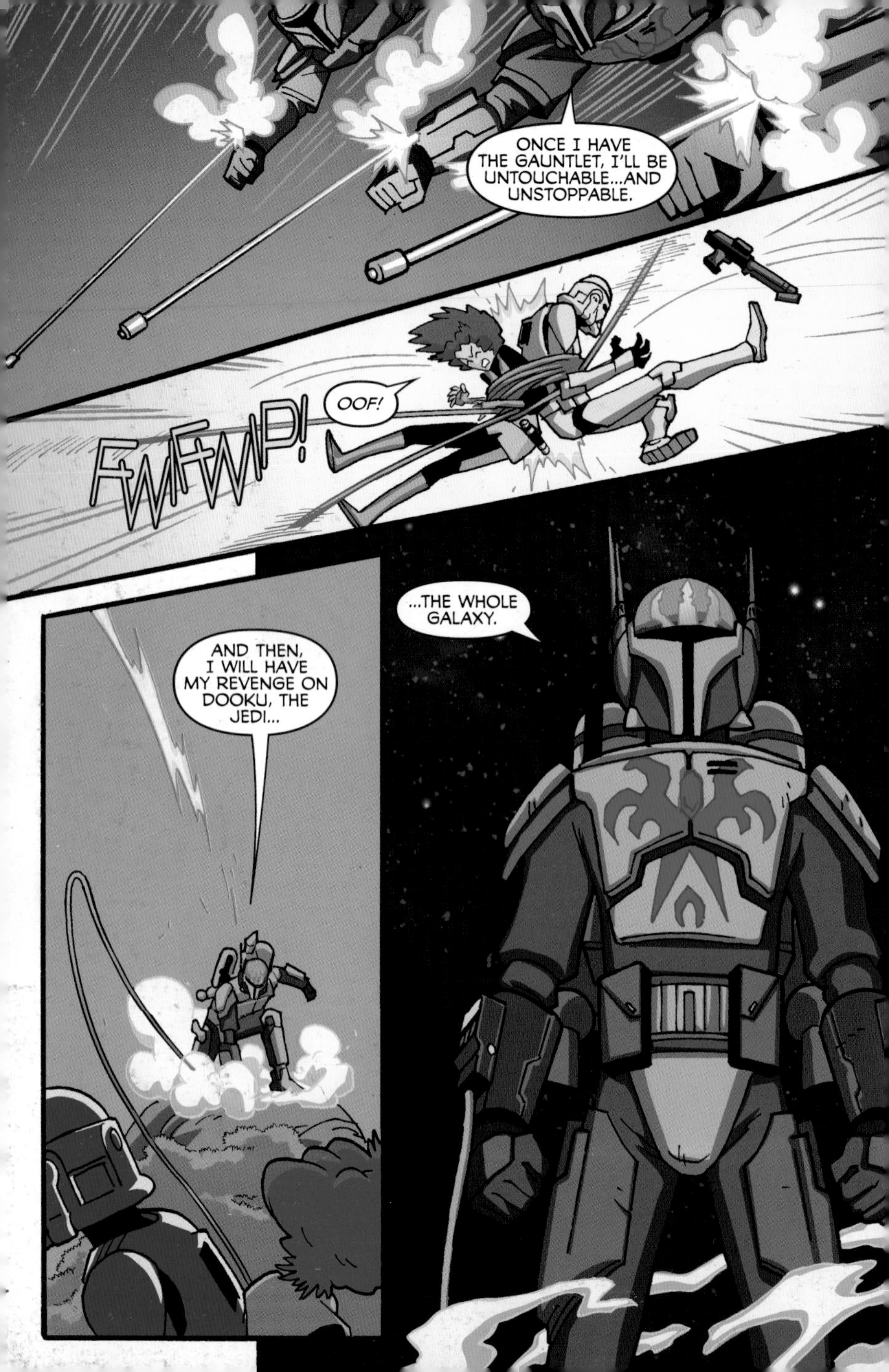
ONCE I HAVE THE GAUNTLET, I'LL BE UNTOUCHABLE...AND UNSTOPPABLE.
OOF!
FWIFWIP!
AND THEN, I WILL HAVE MY REVENGE ON DOOKU, THE JEDI...
...THE WHOLE GALAXY.

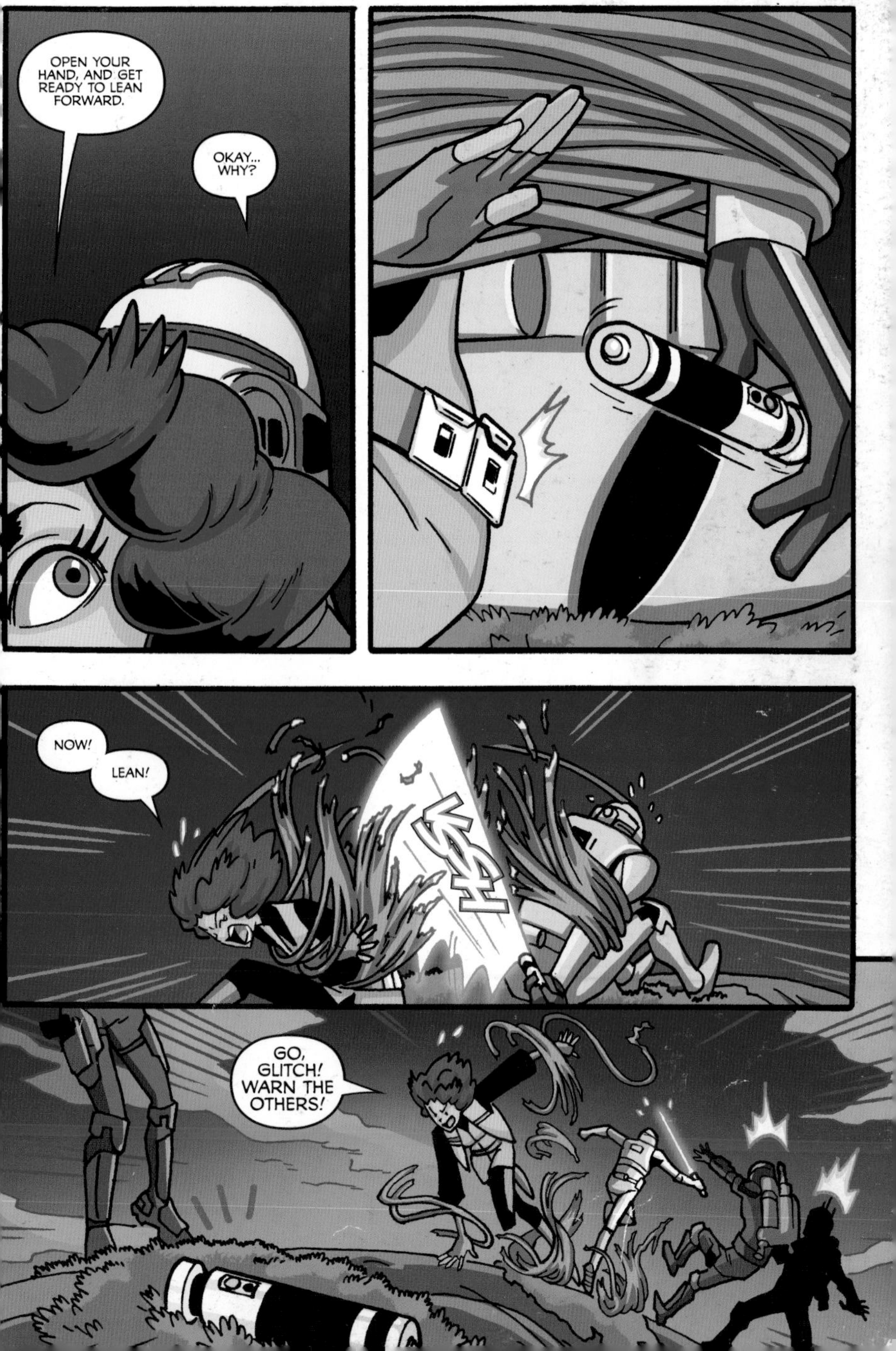
OPEN YOUR HAND, AND GET READY TO LEAN FORWARD.
OKAY... WHY?
NOW!
LEAN!
VSSH
GO, GLITCH! WARN THE OTHERS!

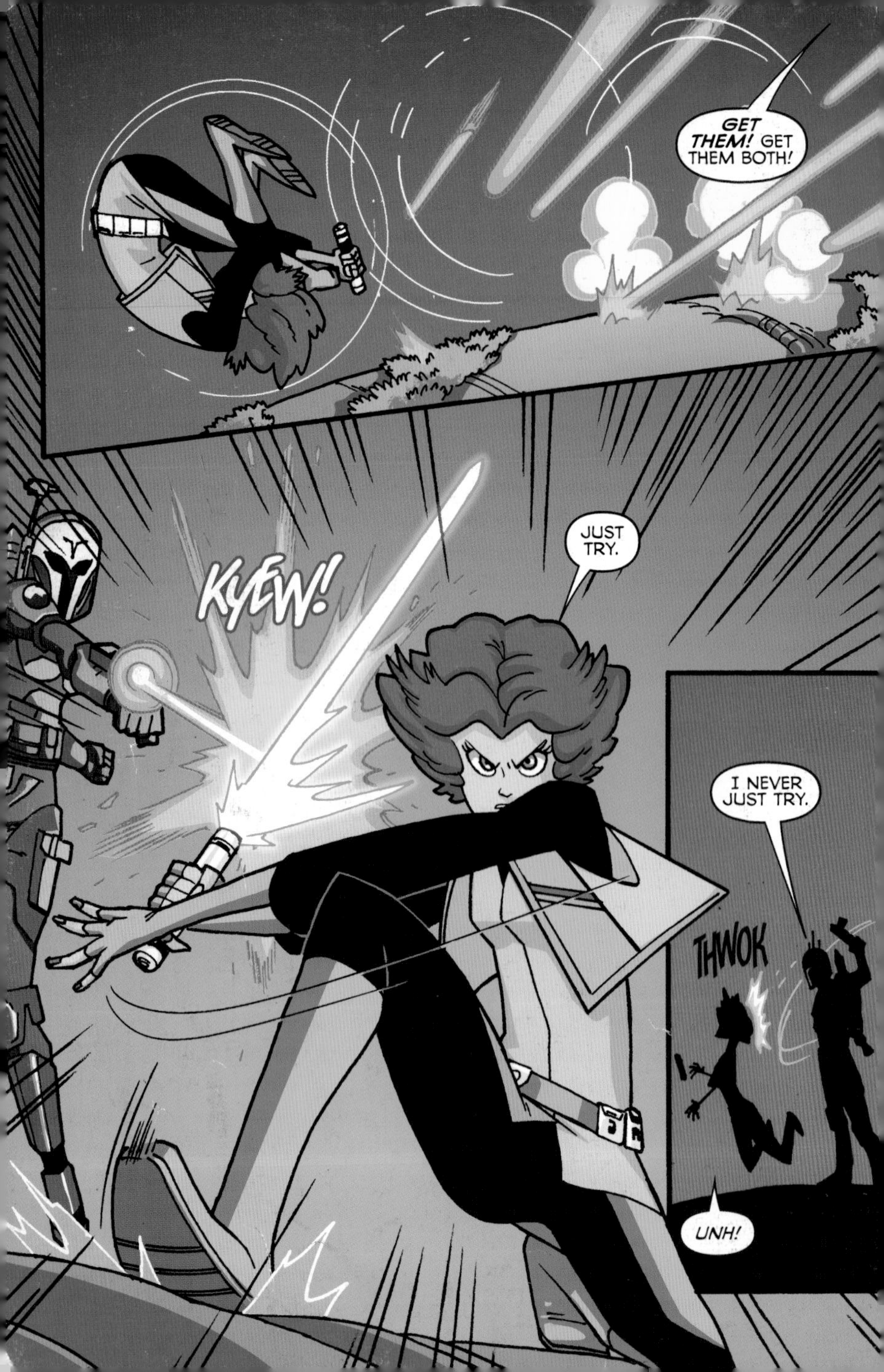
GET THEM! GET THEM BOTH!
JUST TRY.
KYEW!
I NEVER JUST TRY.
THWOK
UNH!

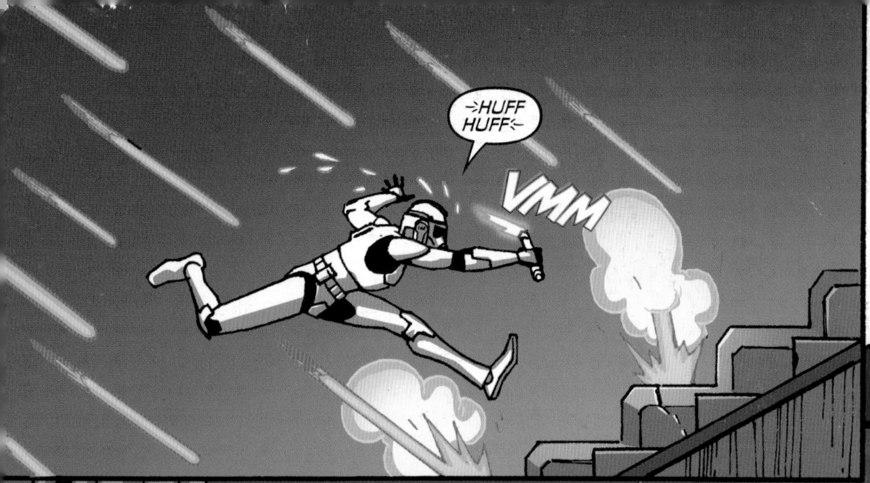
HUFF HUFF
VMM
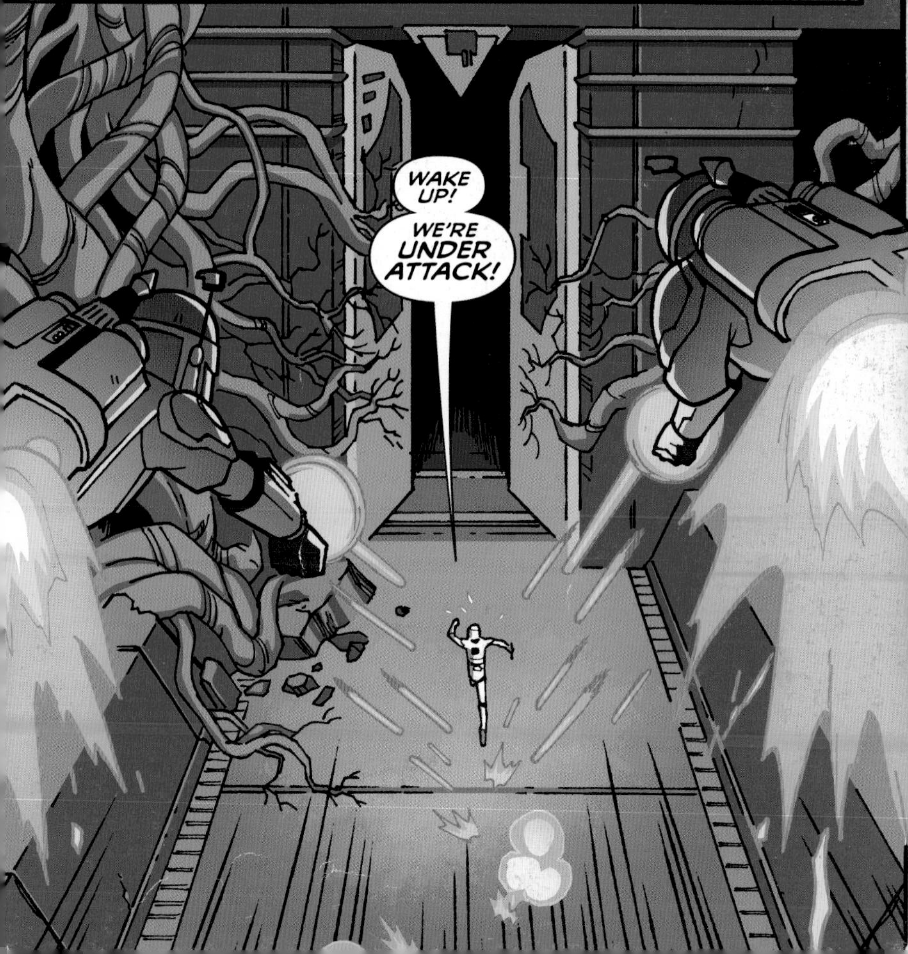
WAKE UP!
WE'RE UNDER ATTACK!

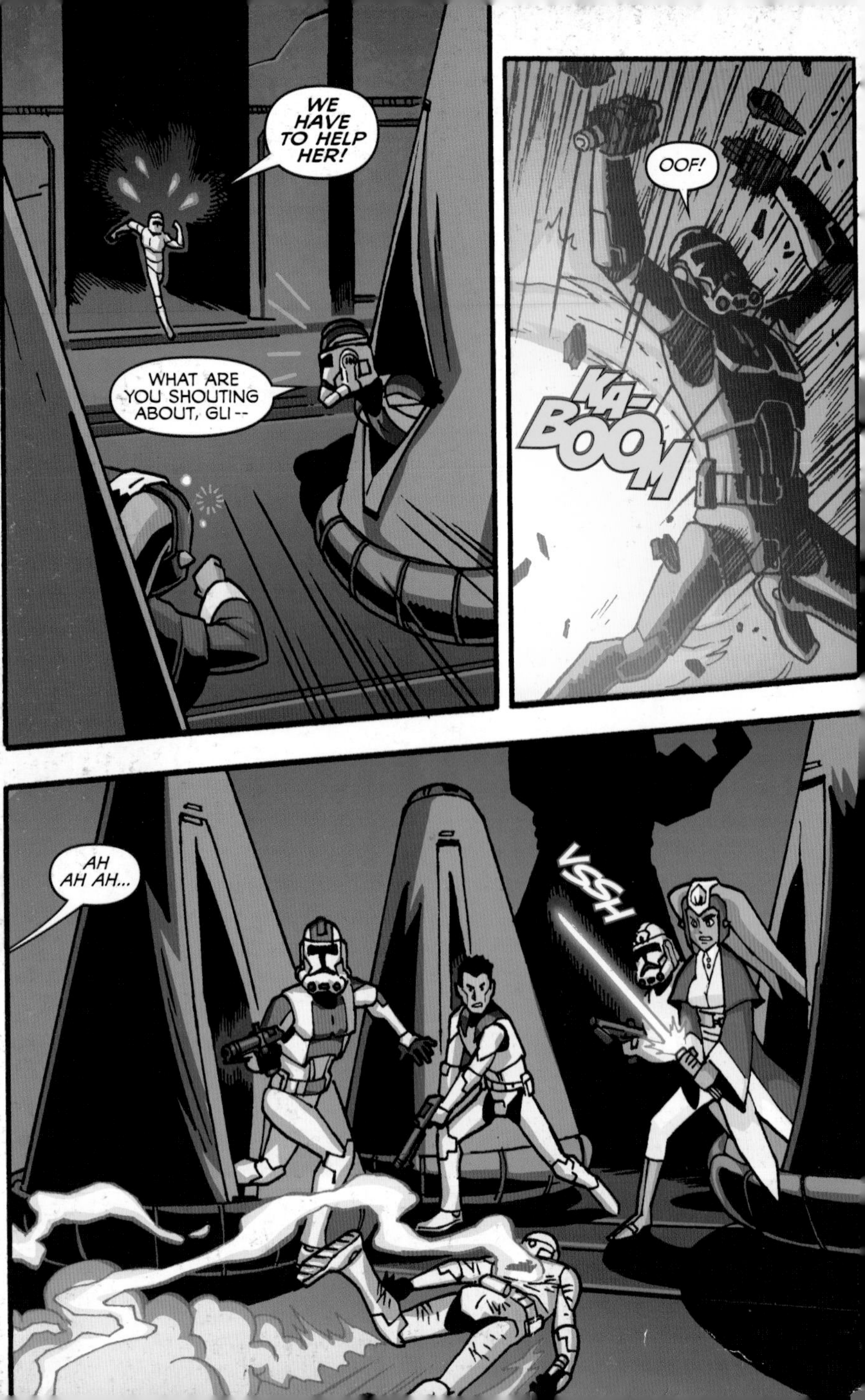
WE HAVE TO HELP HER!
WHAT ARE YOU SHOUTING ABOUT, GLI --
OOF!
KA-BOOM
AH AH AH...
VSSH

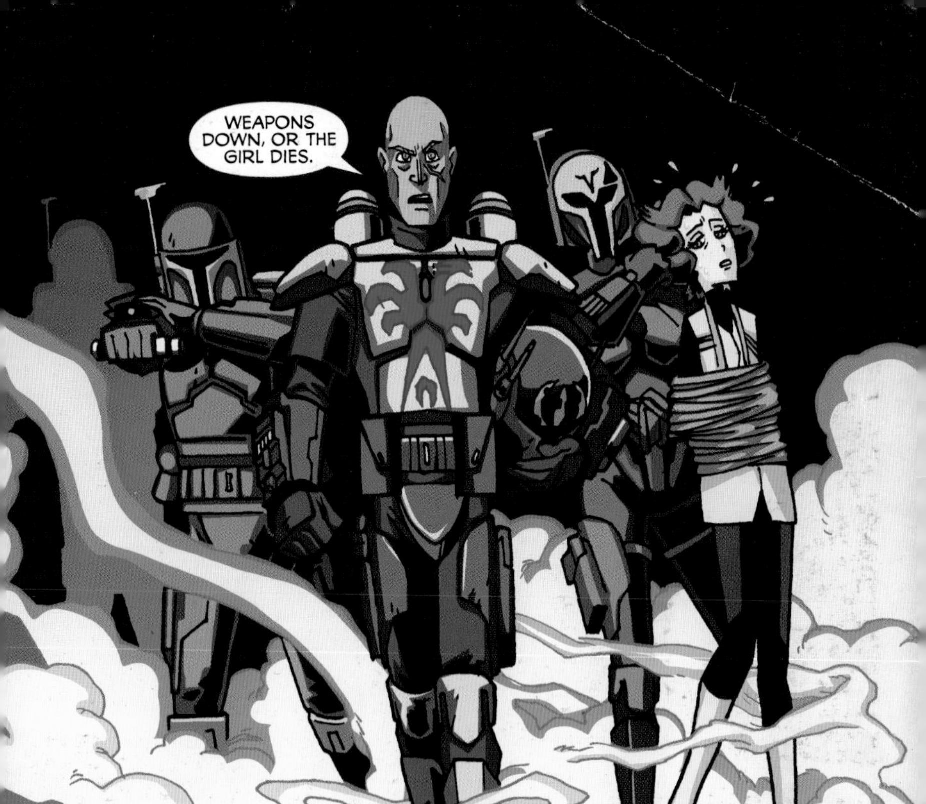
WEAPONS DOWN, OR THE GIRL DIES.

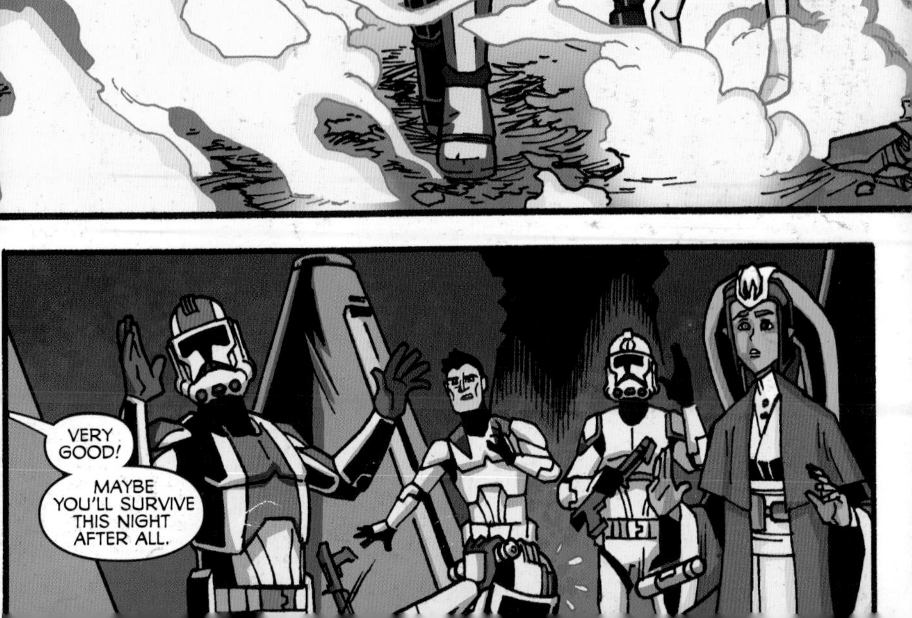
VERY GOOD!
MAYBE YOU'LL SURVIVE THIS NIGHT AFTER ALL.

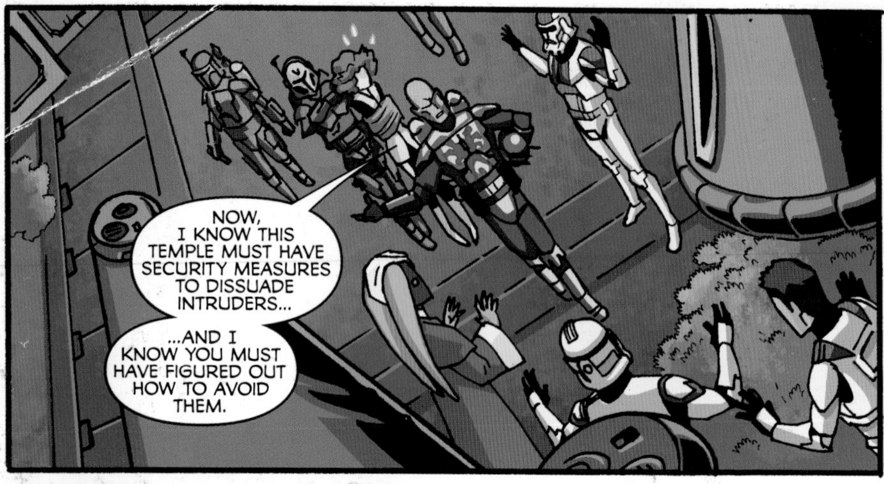
NOW, I KNOW THIS TEMPLE MUST HAVE SECURITY MEASURES TO DISSUADE INTRUDERS...
...AND I KNOW YOU MUST HAVE FIGURED OUT HOW TO AVOID THEM.

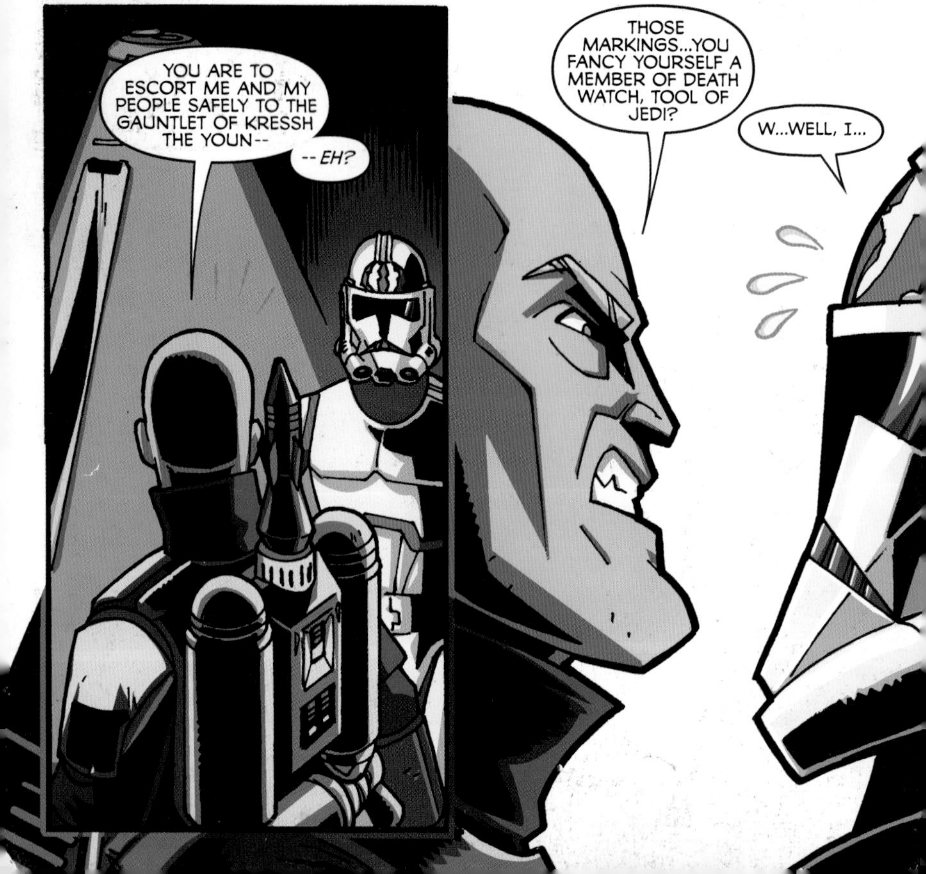
YOU ARE TO ESCORT ME AND MY PEOPLE SAFELY TO THE GAUNTLET OF KRESSH THE YOUN--
--EH?
THOSE MARKINGS...YOU FANCY YOURSELF A MEMBER OF DEATH WATCH, TOOL OF JEDI?
W...WELL, I...

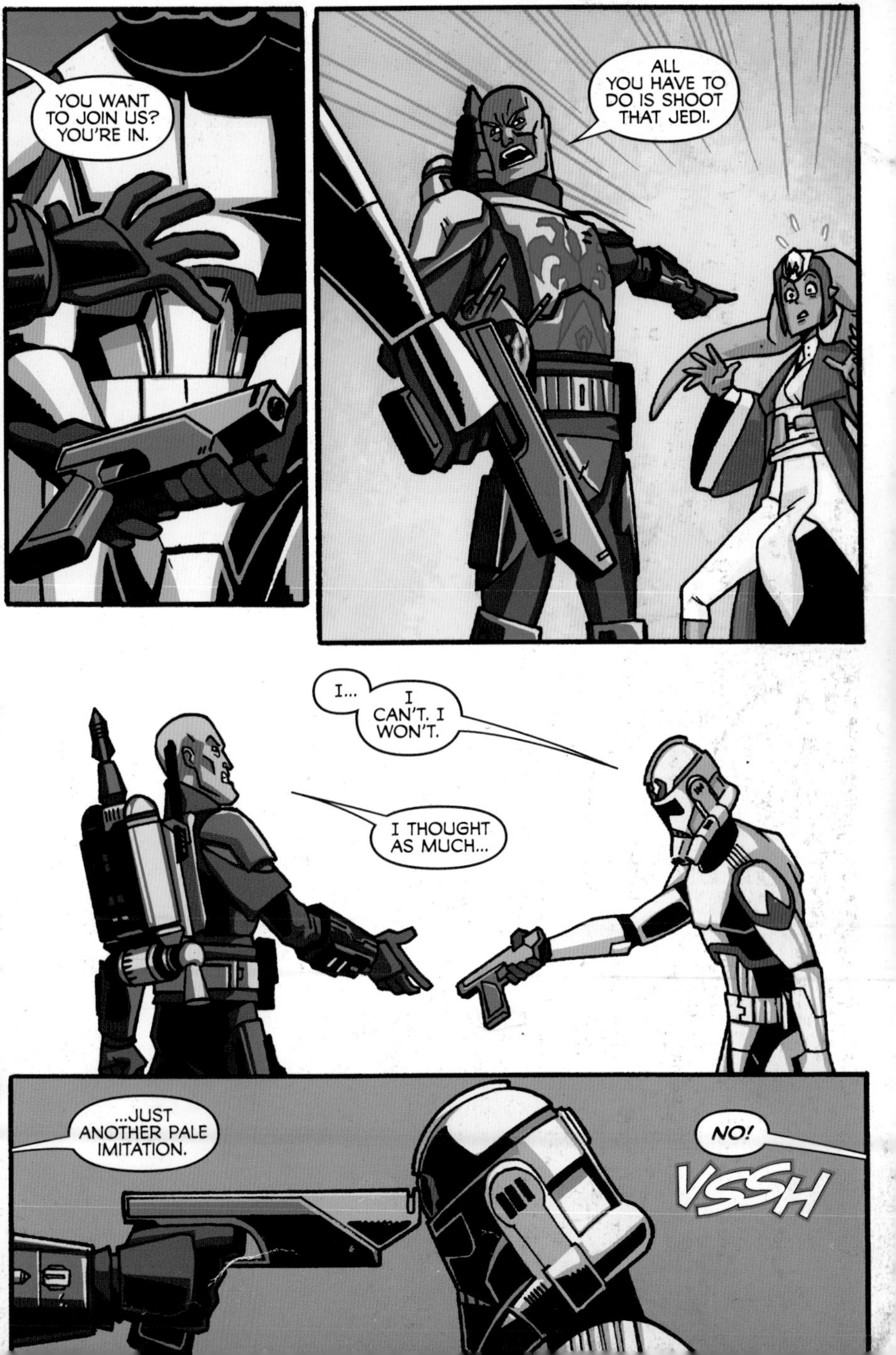
YOU WANT TO JOIN US? YOU'RE IN.
ALL YOU HAVE TO DO IS SHOOT THAT JEDI.
I...
I CAN'T. I WON'T.
I THOUGHT AS MUCH...
...JUST ANOTHER PALE IMITATION.
NO!
VSSH

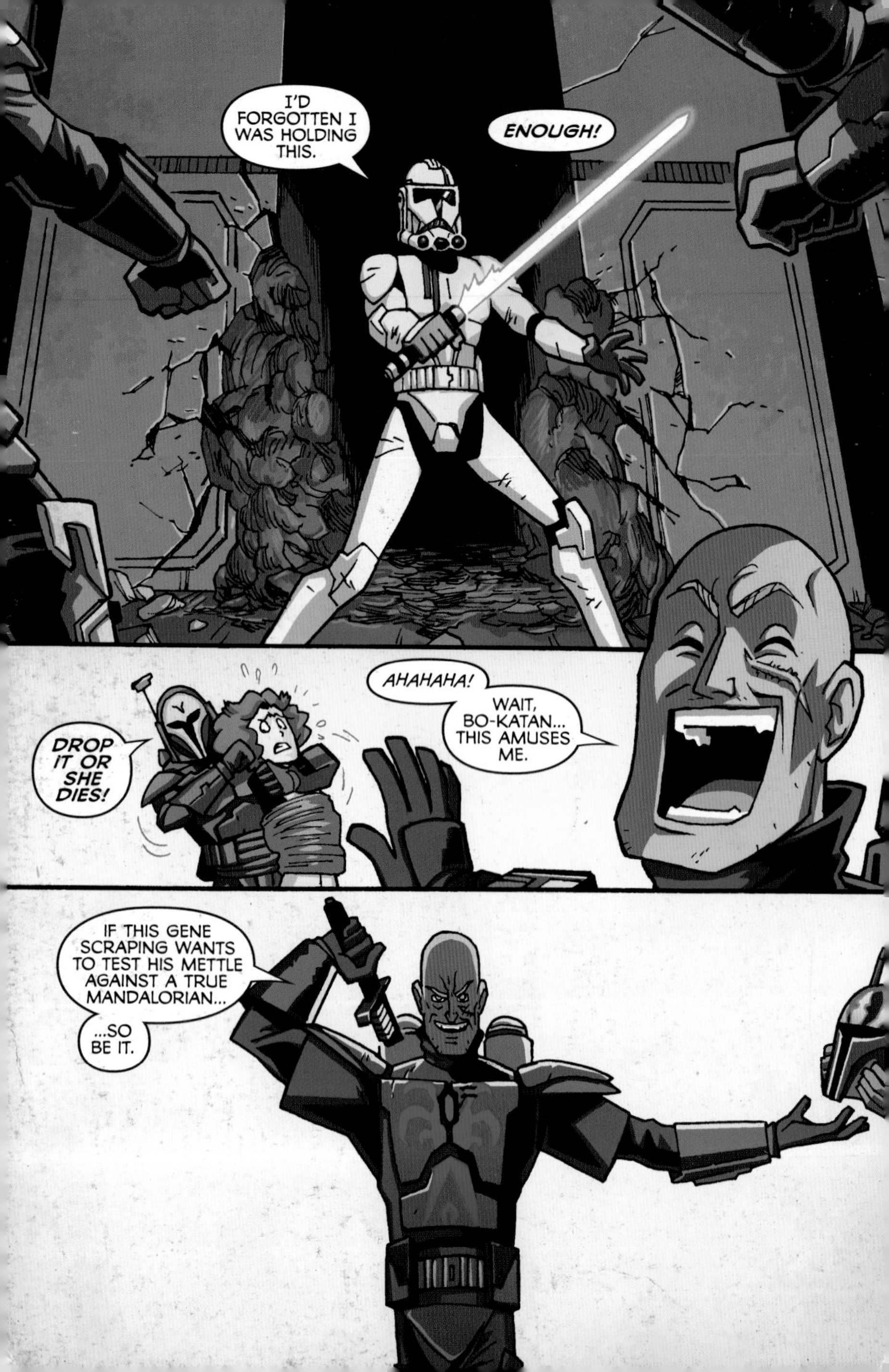
I'D FORGOTTEN I WAS HOLDING THIS.
ENOUGH!
DROP IT OR SHE DIES!
AHAHAHA!
WAIT, BO-KATAN... THIS AMUSES ME.
IF THIS GENE SCRAPING WANTS TO TEST HIS METTLE AGAINST A TRUE MANDALORIAN...
...SO BE IT.

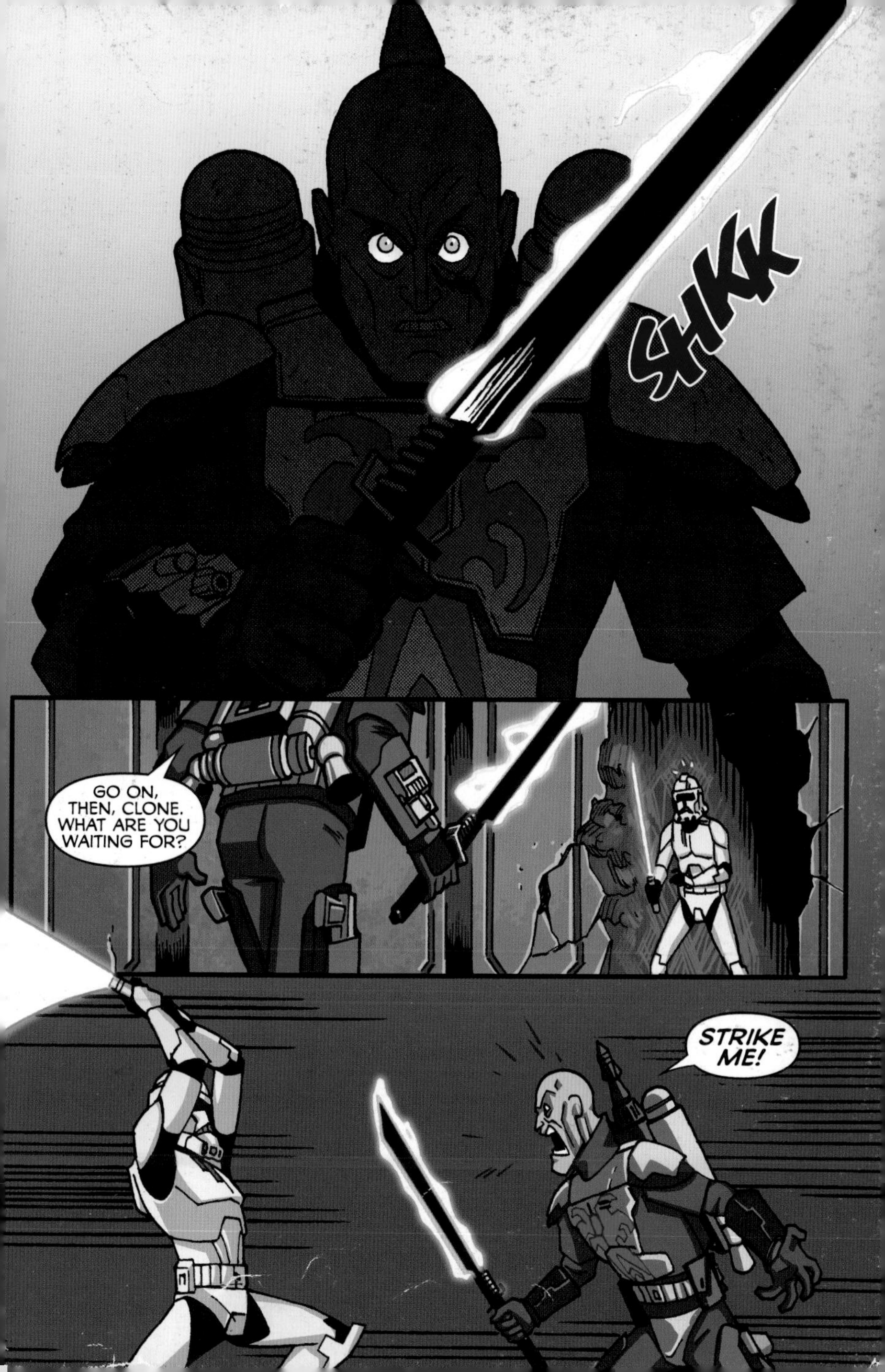
SHKK
GO ON, THEN, CLONE. WHAT ARE YOU WAITING FOR?
STRIKE ME!

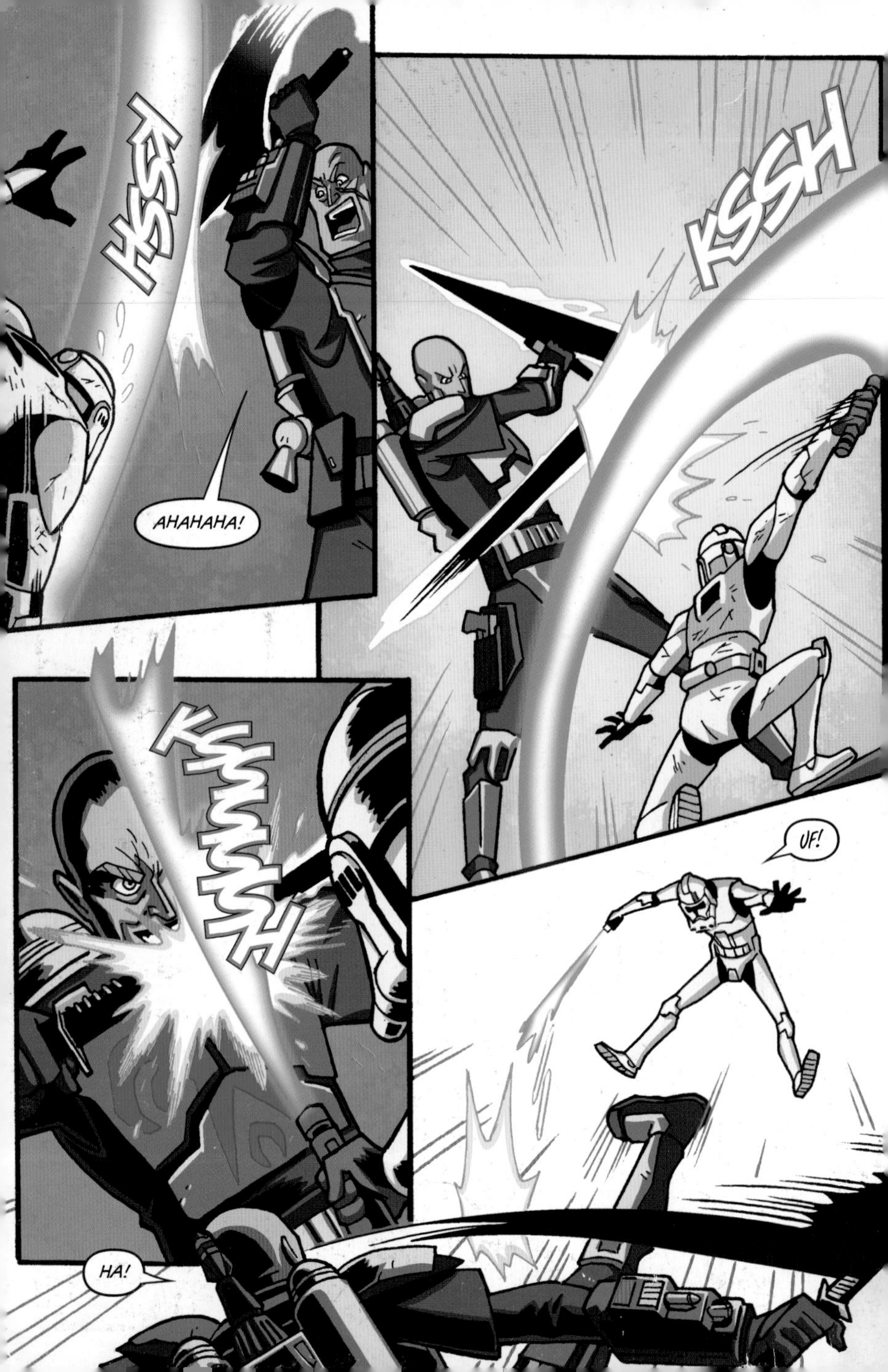
KSSH
AHAHAHA!
KSSH
UF!
HA!

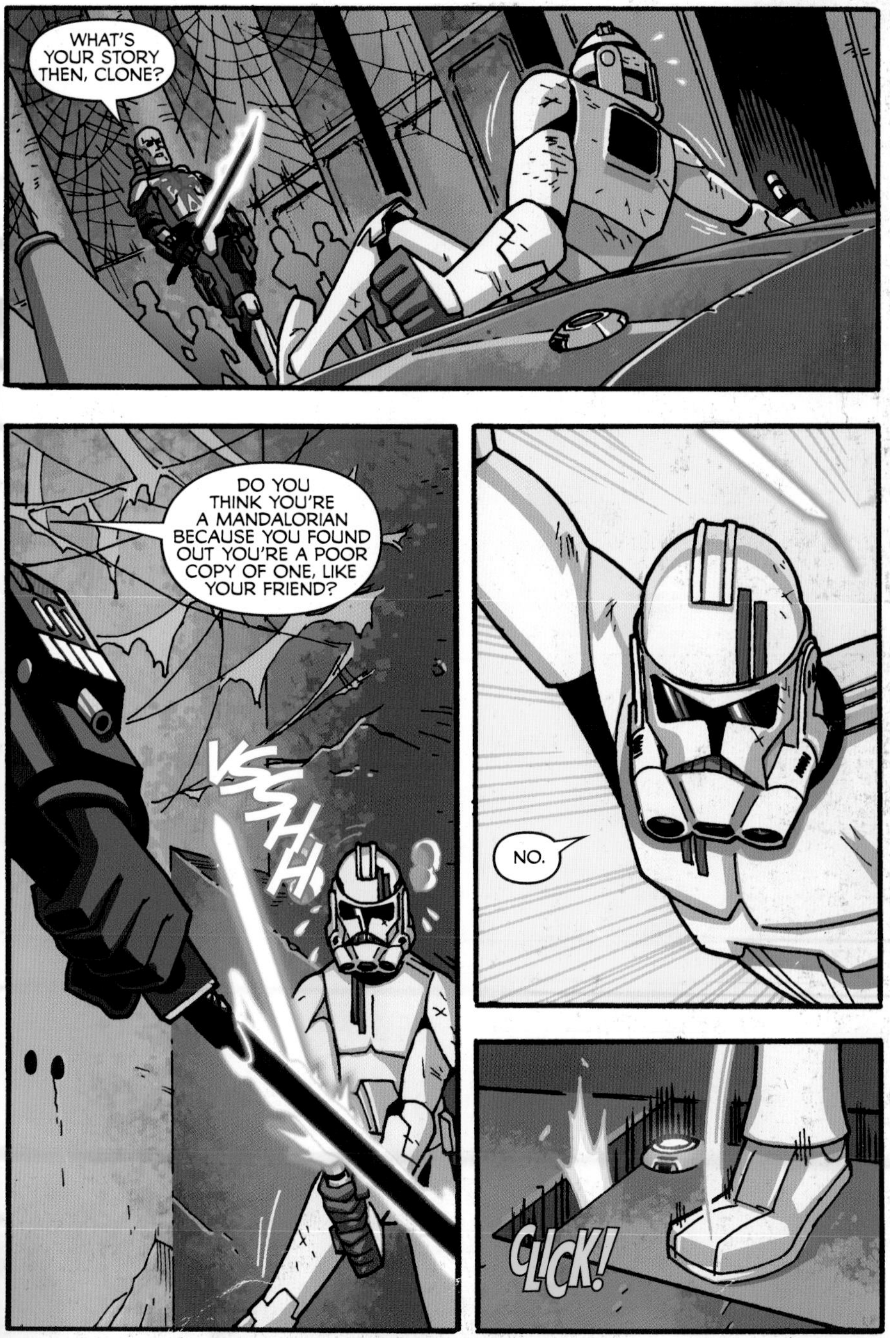
WHAT'S YOUR STORY THEN, CLONE?
DO YOU THINK YOU'RE A MANDALORIAN BECAUSE YOU FOUND OUT YOU'RE A POOR COPY OF ONE, LIKE YOUR FRIEND?
VSSHH
NO.
CLICK!

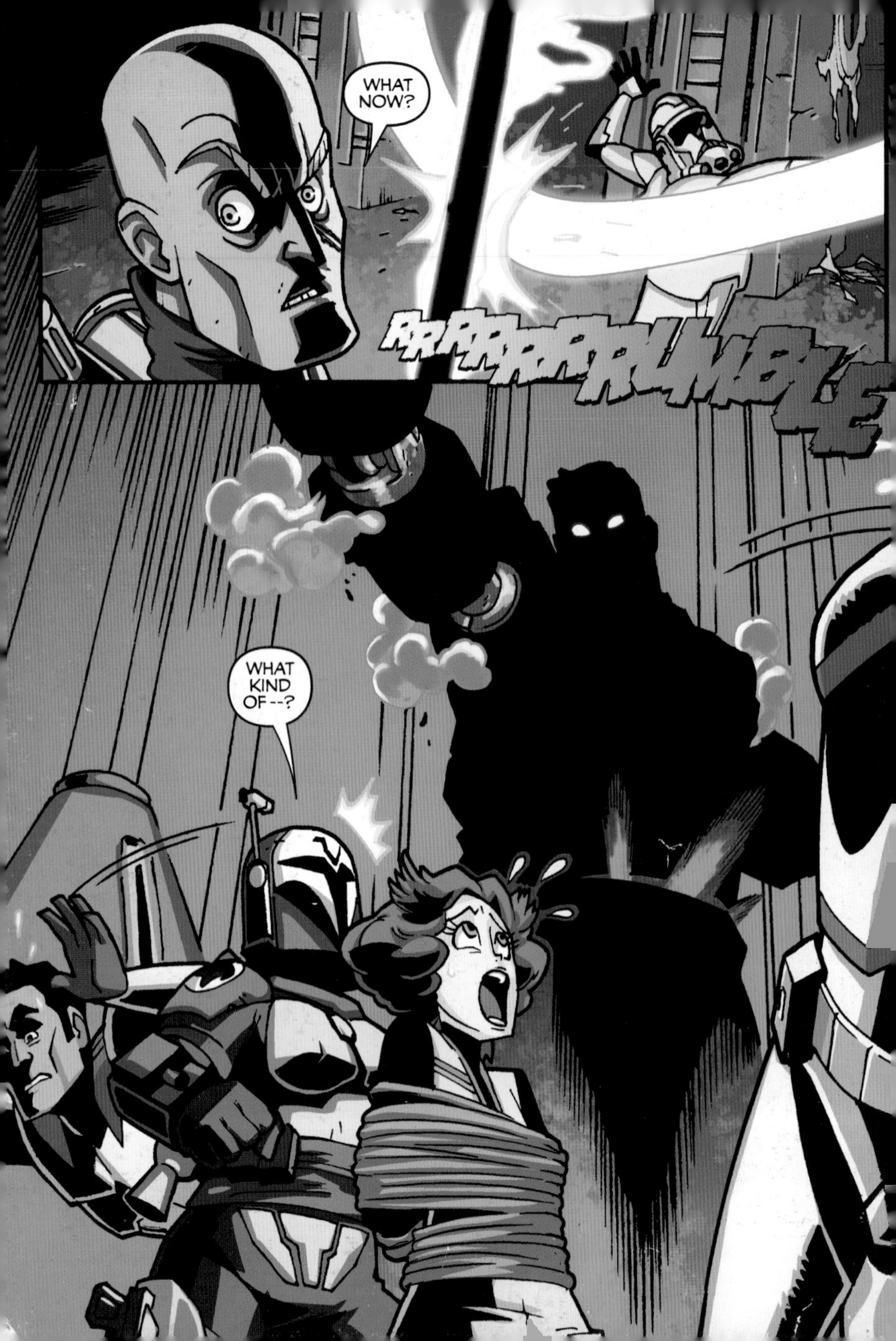
WHAT NOW?
RRRRRRRRRUMBLE
WHAT KIND OF --?

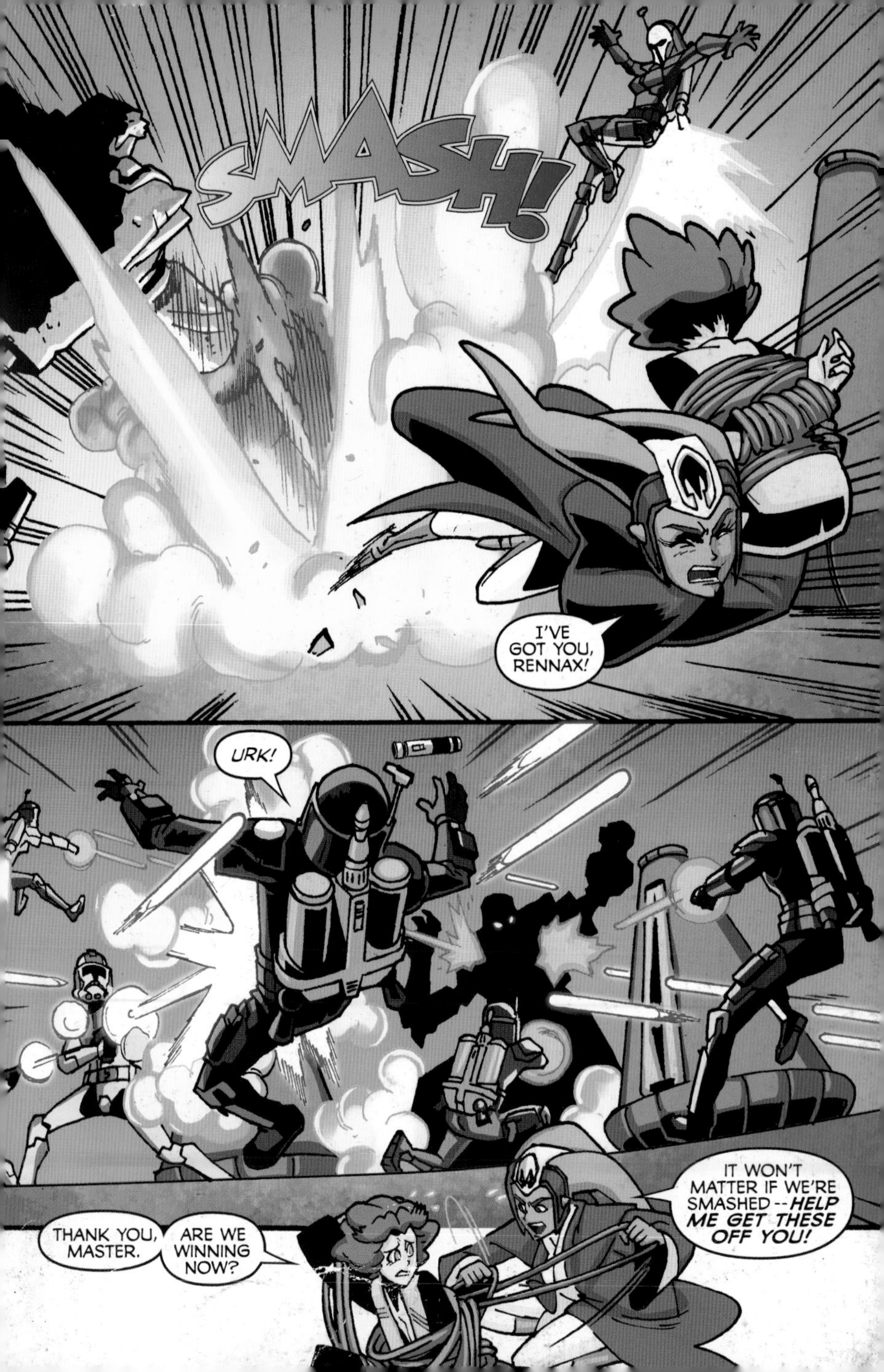
SMASH!
I'VE GOT YOU, RENNAX!
URK!
IT WON'T MATTER IF WE'RE SMASHED--HELP ME GET THESE OFF YOU!
THANK YOU, MASTER.
ARE WE WINNING NOW?

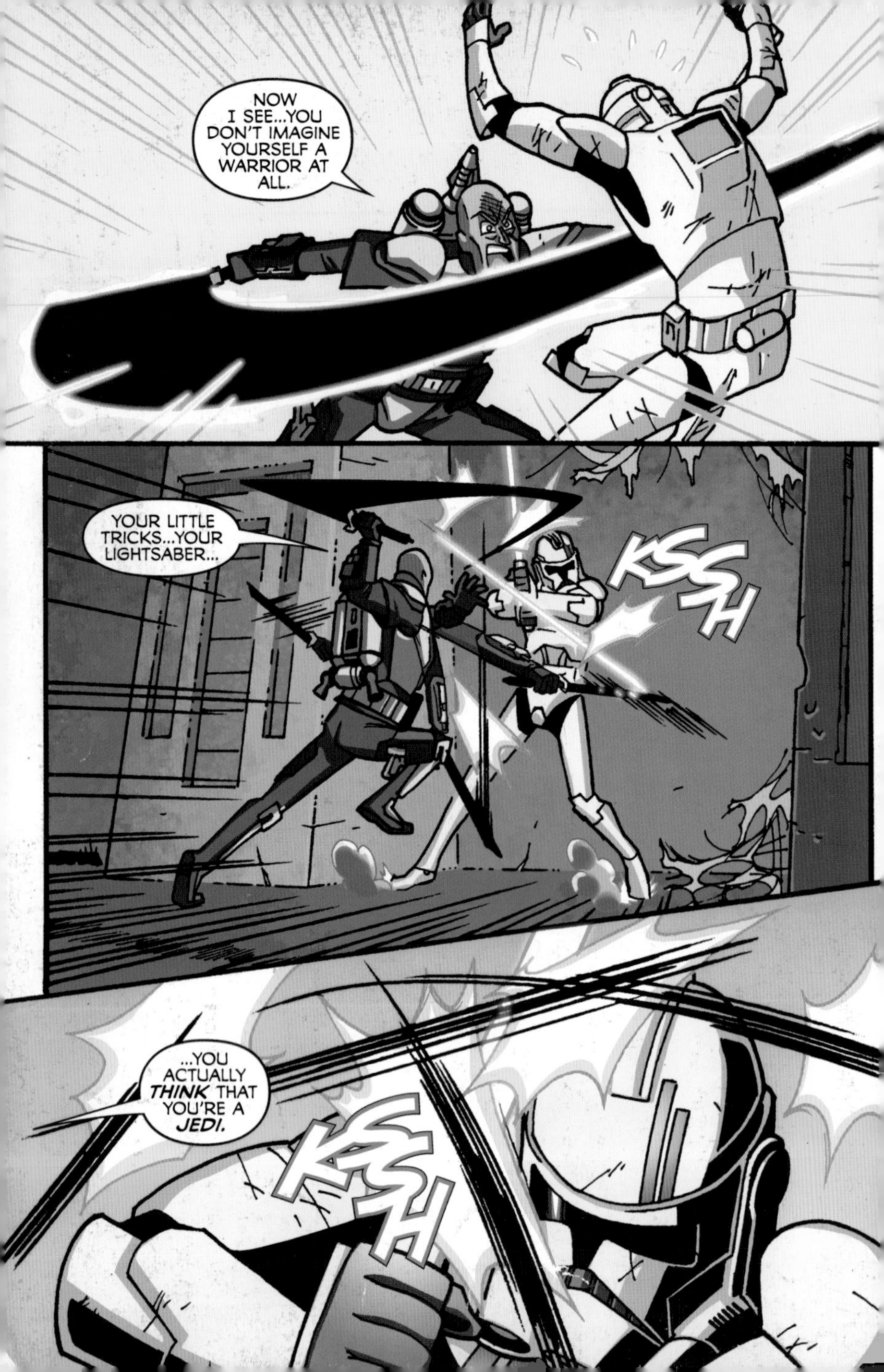
NOW I SEE...YOU DON'T IMAGINE YOURSELF A WARRIOR AT ALL.
YOUR LITTLE TRICKS...YOUR LIGHTSABER...
KSSSH
...YOU ACTUALLY *THINK* THAT YOU'RE A *JEDI.*
KSSH

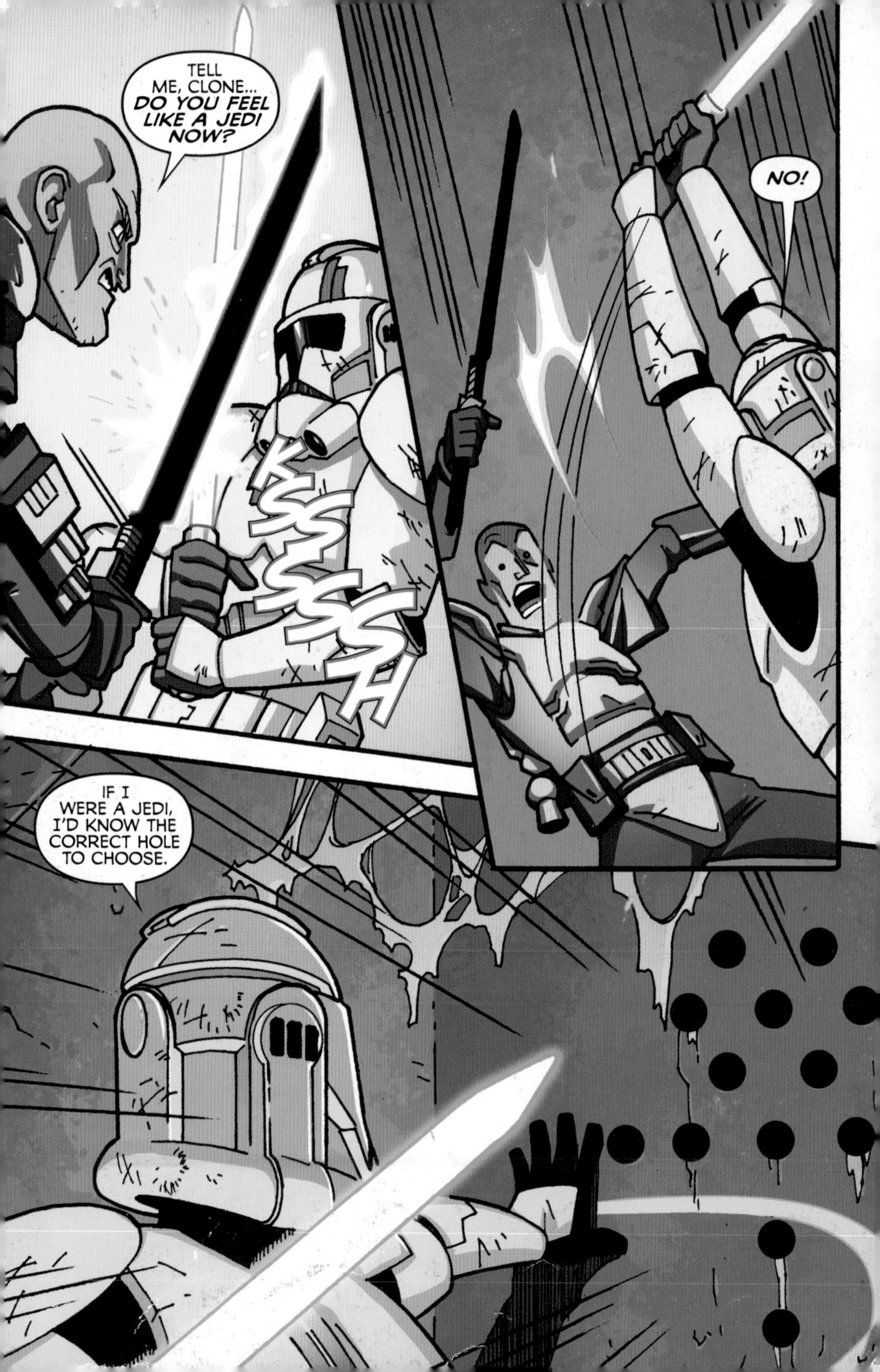
TELL ME, CLONE... *DO YOU FEEL LIKE A JEDI NOW?*
KSSSSSSH
NO!
IF I WERE A JEDI, I'D KNOW THE CORRECT HOLE TO CHOOSE.

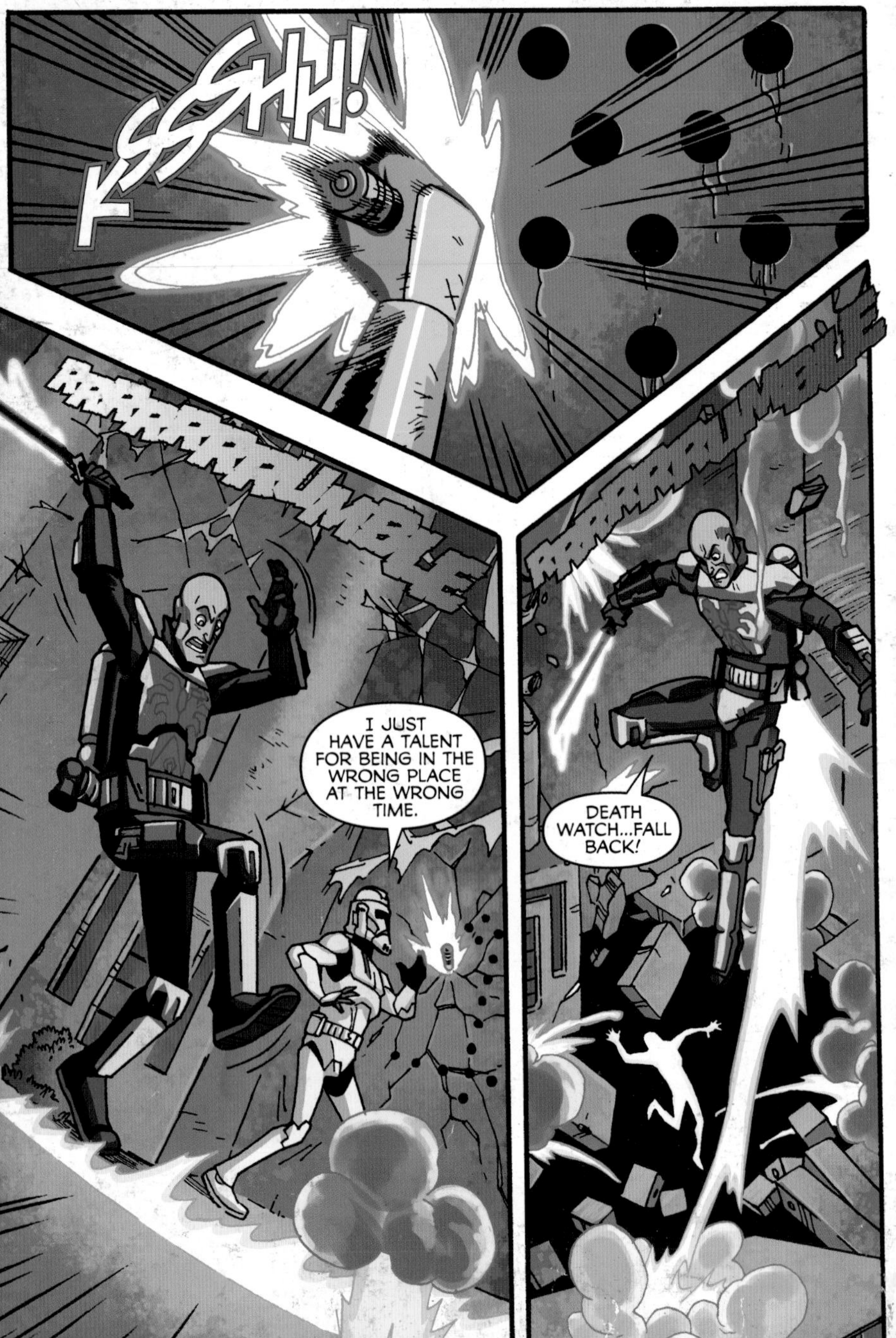
KSSHH!
I JUST HAVE A TALENT FOR BEING IN THE WRONG PLACE AT THE WRONG TIME.
DEATH WATCH...FALL BACK!

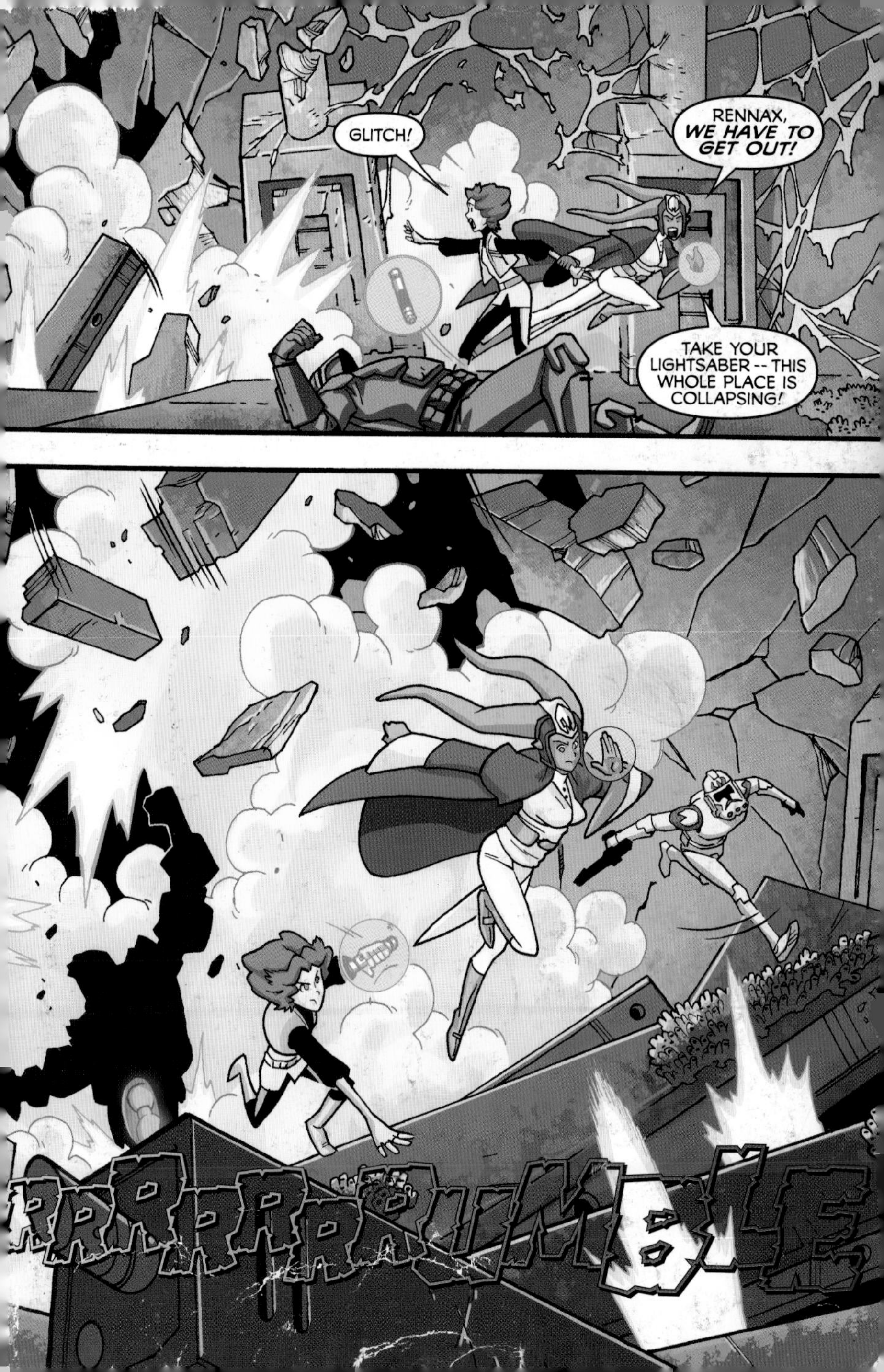
GLITCH!
RENNAX, *WE HAVE TO GET OUT!*
TAKE YOUR LIGHTSABER -- THIS WHOLE PLACE IS COLLAPSING!
RRRRRUMBLE

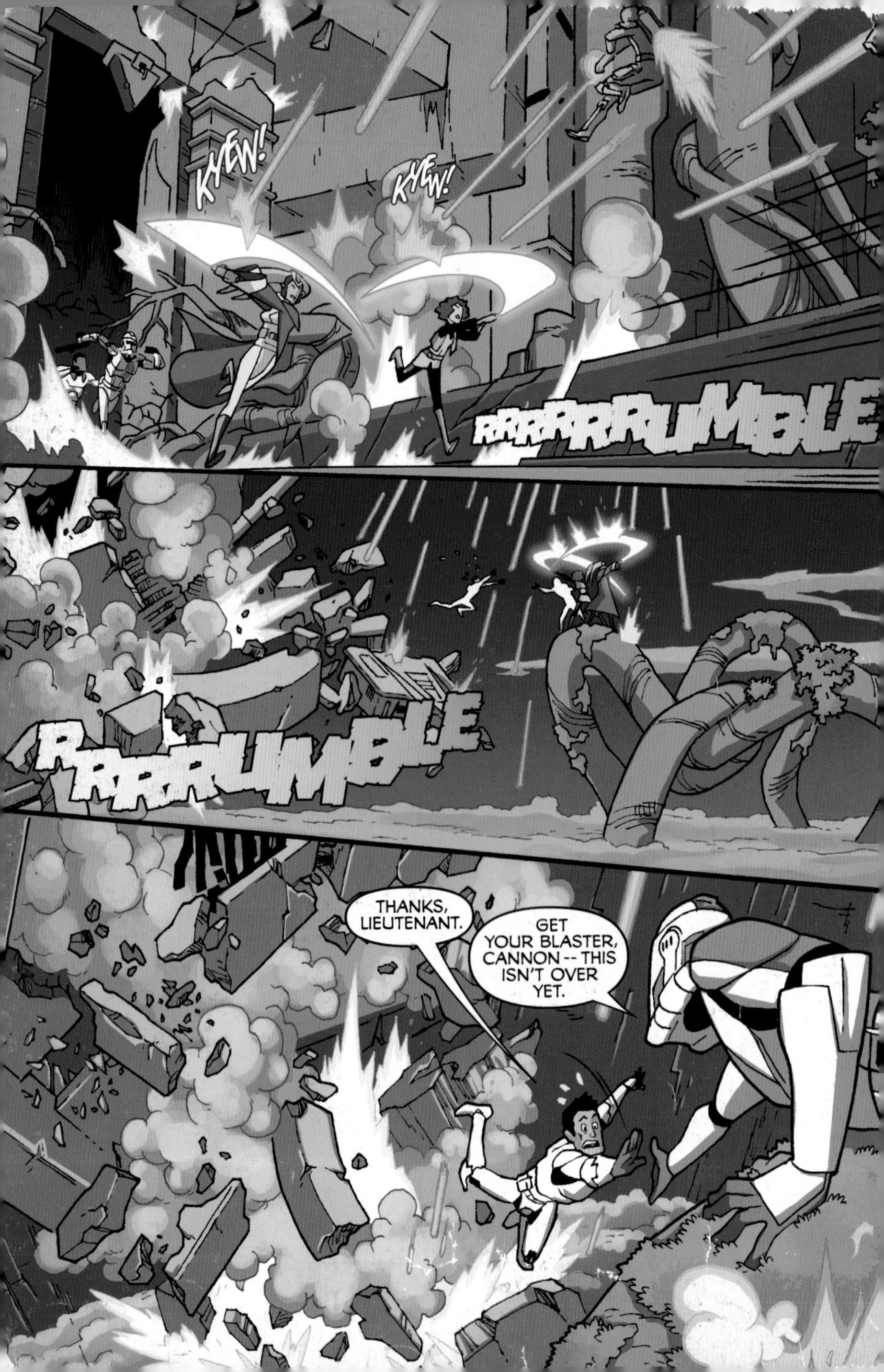
KYEW!
KYEW!
RRRRRRRUMBLE
RRRRRUMBLE
THANKS, LIEUTENANT.
GET YOUR BLASTER, CANNON -- THIS ISN'T OVER YET.

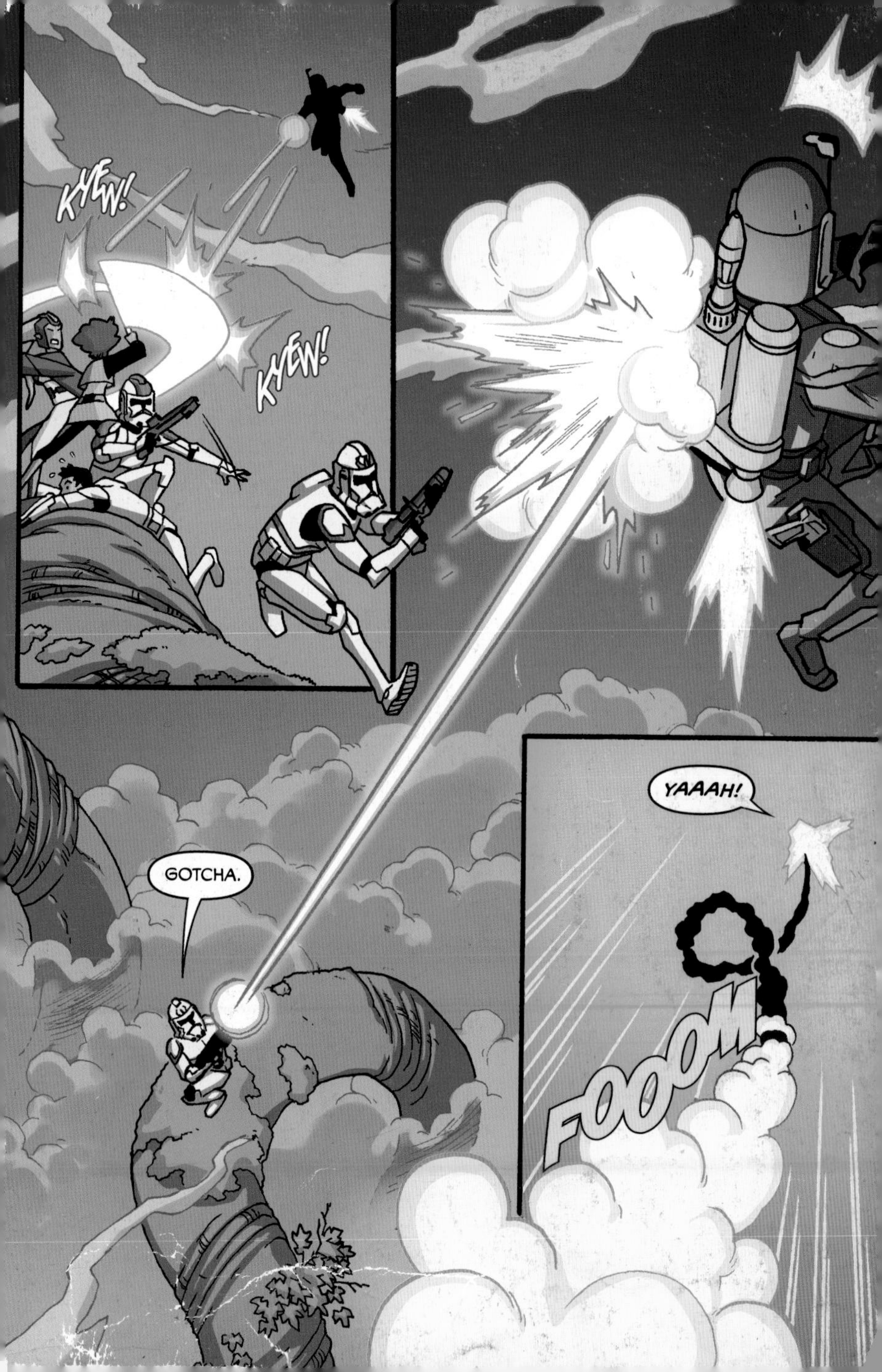
KYEW!
KYEW!
GOTCHA.
YAAAH!
FOOOM

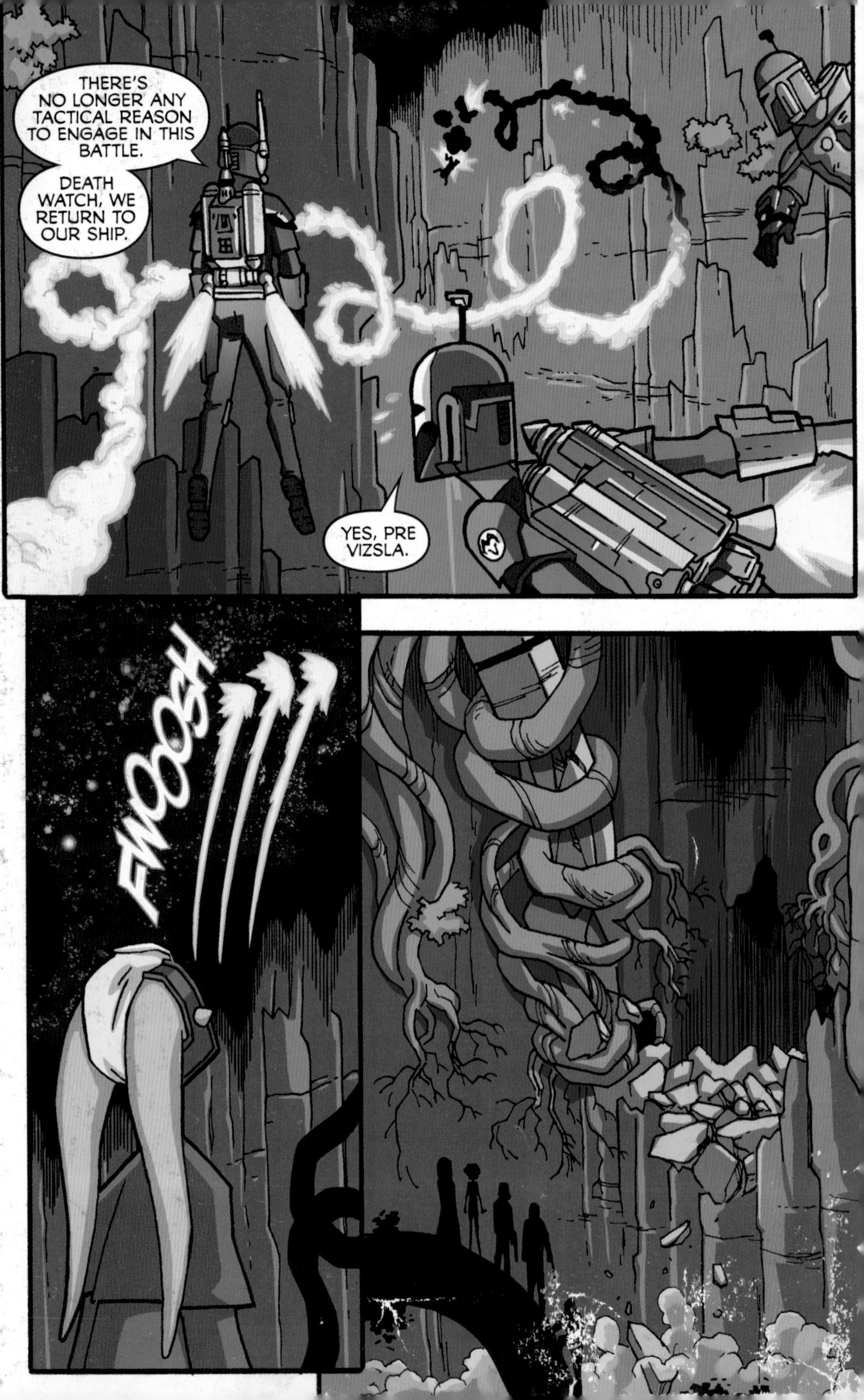
THERE'S NO LONGER ANY TACTICAL REASON TO ENGAGE IN THIS BATTLE.
DEATH WATCH, WE RETURN TO OUR SHIP.
YES, PRE VIZSLA.
FWOOOSH

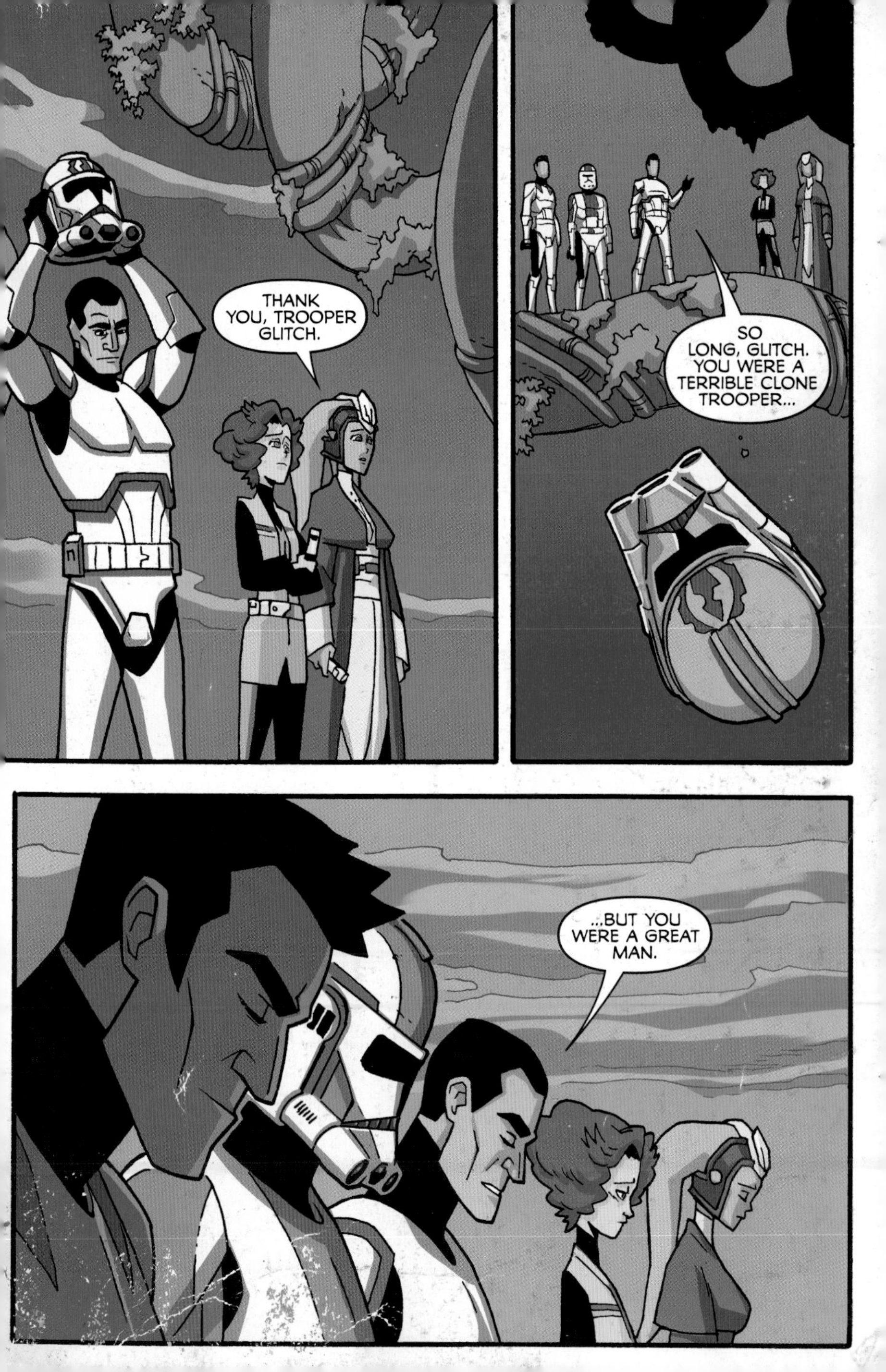
THANK YOU, TROOPER GLITCH.
SO LONG, GLITCH. YOU WERE A TERRIBLE CLONE TROOPER...
...BUT YOU WERE A GREAT MAN.

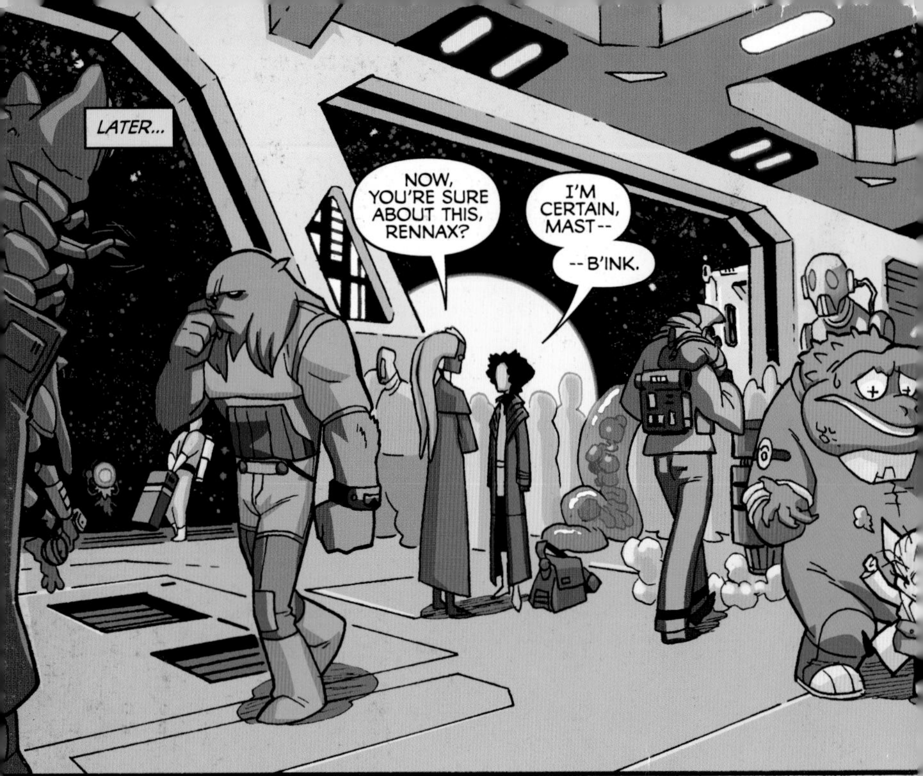
LATER...
NOW, YOU'RE SURE ABOUT THIS, RENNAX?
I'M CERTAIN, MAST--
--B'INK.

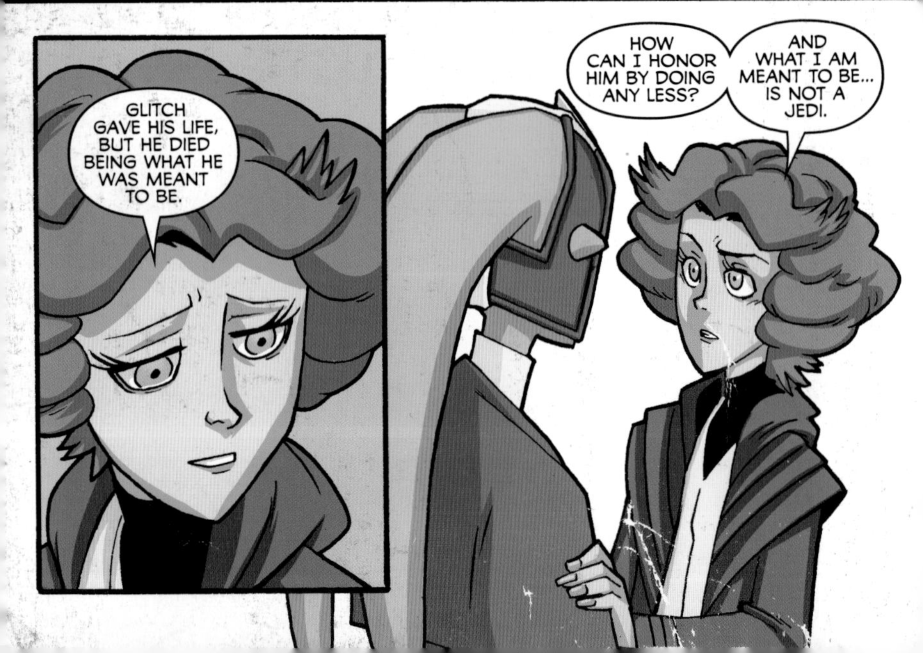
GLITCH GAVE HIS LIFE, BUT HE DIED BEING WHAT HE WAS MEANT TO BE.
HOW CAN I HONOR HIM BY DOING ANY LESS?
AND WHAT I AM MEANT TO BE... IS NOT A JEDI.

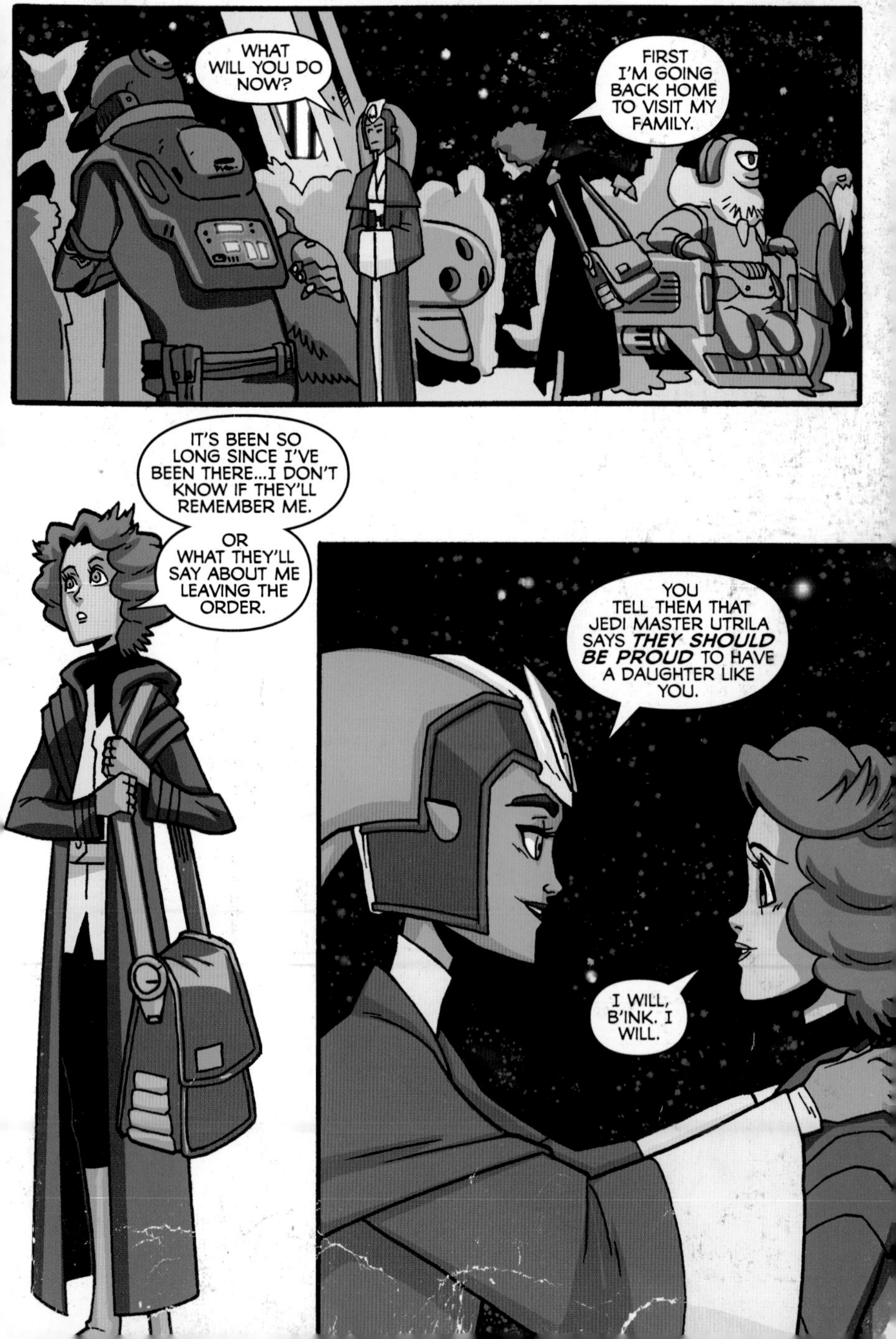
WHAT WILL YOU DO NOW?
FIRST I'M GOING BACK HOME TO VISIT MY FAMILY.
IT'S BEEN SO LONG SINCE I'VE BEEN THERE...I DON'T KNOW IF THEY'LL REMEMBER ME.
OR WHAT THEY'LL SAY ABOUT ME LEAVING THE ORDER.
YOU TELL THEM THAT JEDI MASTER UTRILA SAYS *THEY SHOULD BE PROUD* TO HAVE A DAUGHTER LIKE YOU.
I WILL, B'INK. I WILL.

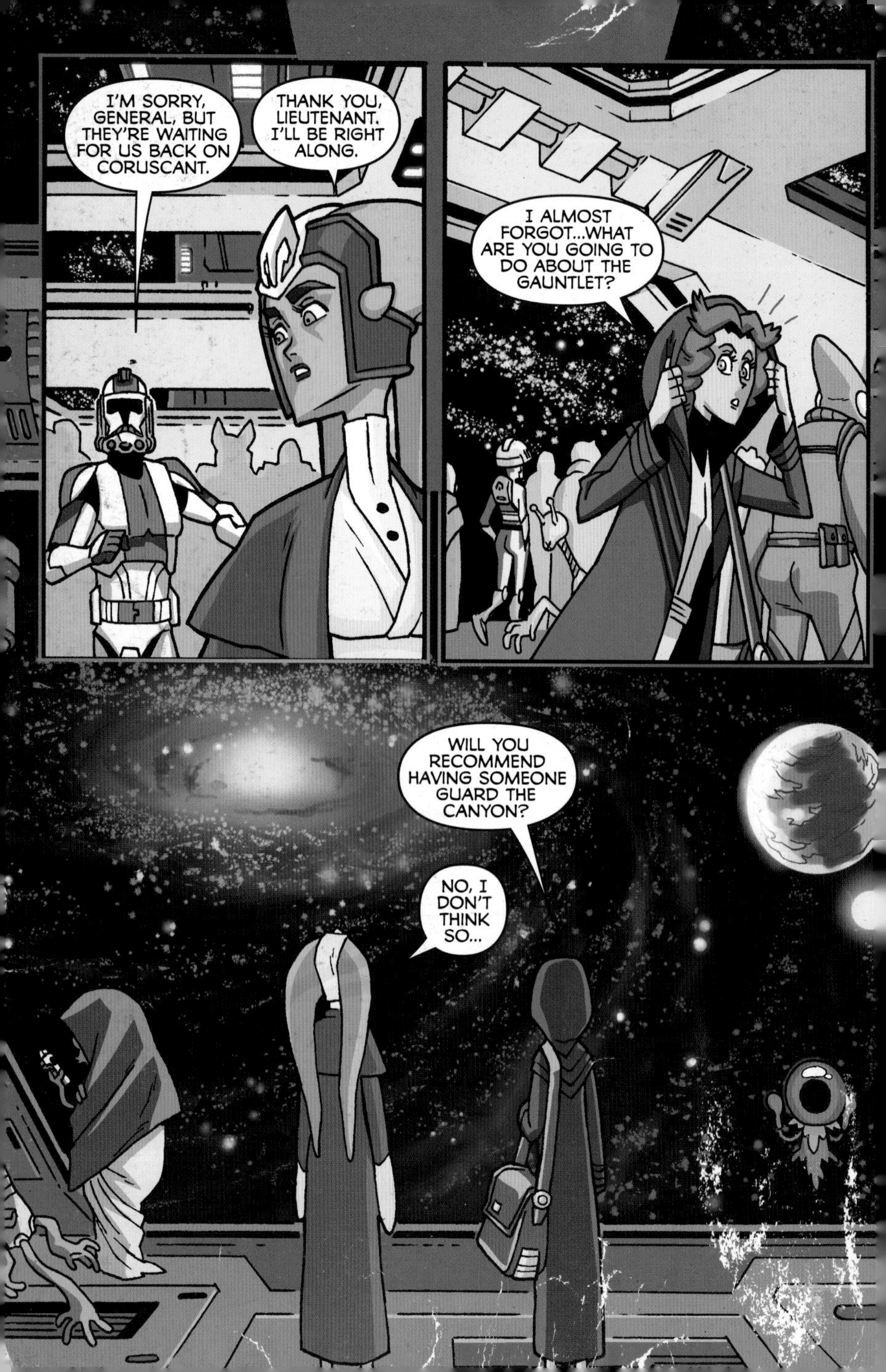
I'M SORRY, GENERAL, BUT THEY'RE WAITING FOR US BACK ON CORUSCANT.
THANK YOU, LIEUTENANT. I'LL BE RIGHT ALONG.
I ALMOST FORGOT...WHAT ARE YOU GOING TO DO ABOUT THE GAUNTLET?
WILL YOU RECOMMEND HAVING SOMEONE GUARD THE CANYON?
NO, I DON'T THINK SO...

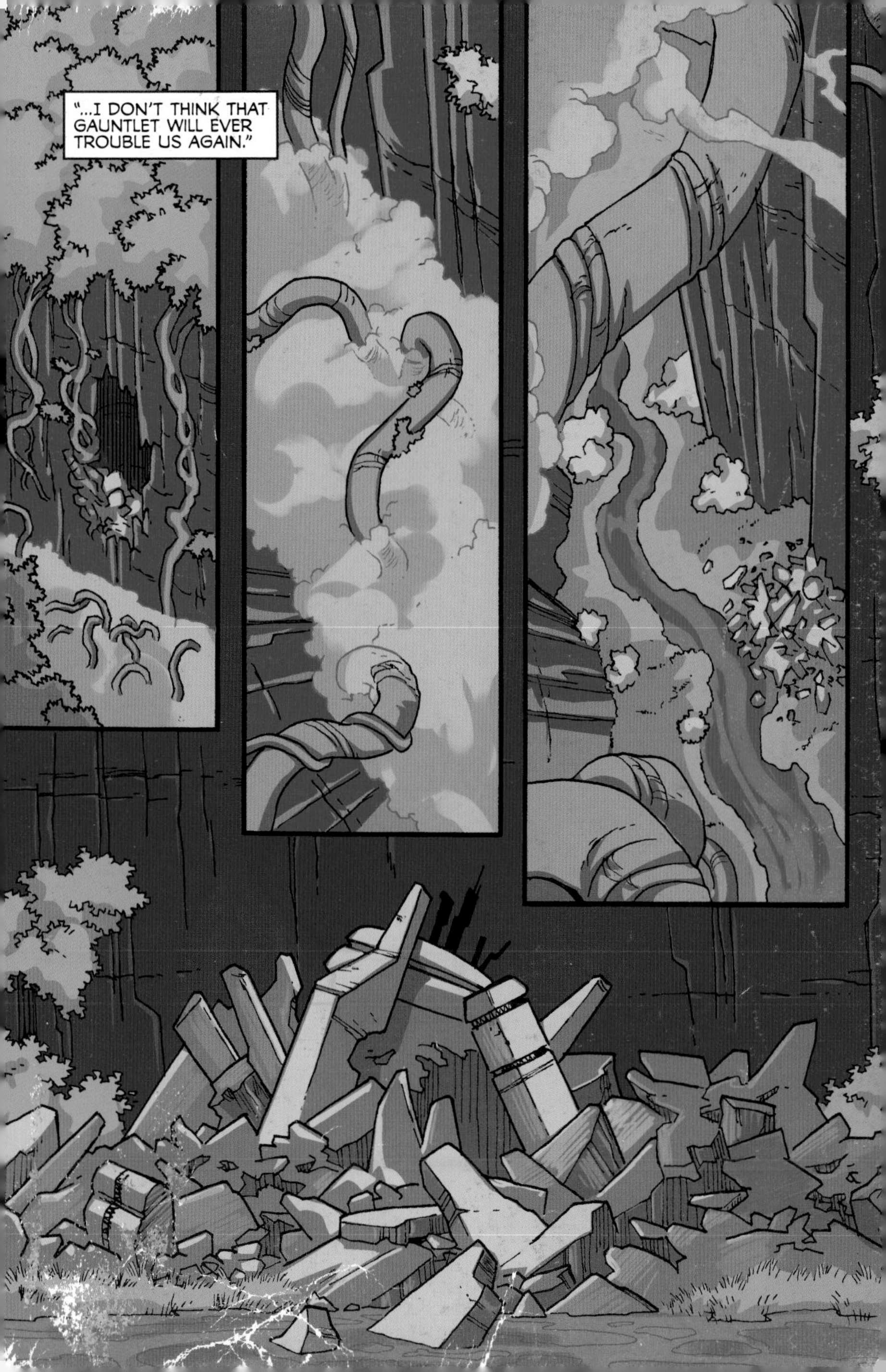
"...I DON'T THINK THAT GAUNTLET WILL EVER TROUBLE US AGAIN."

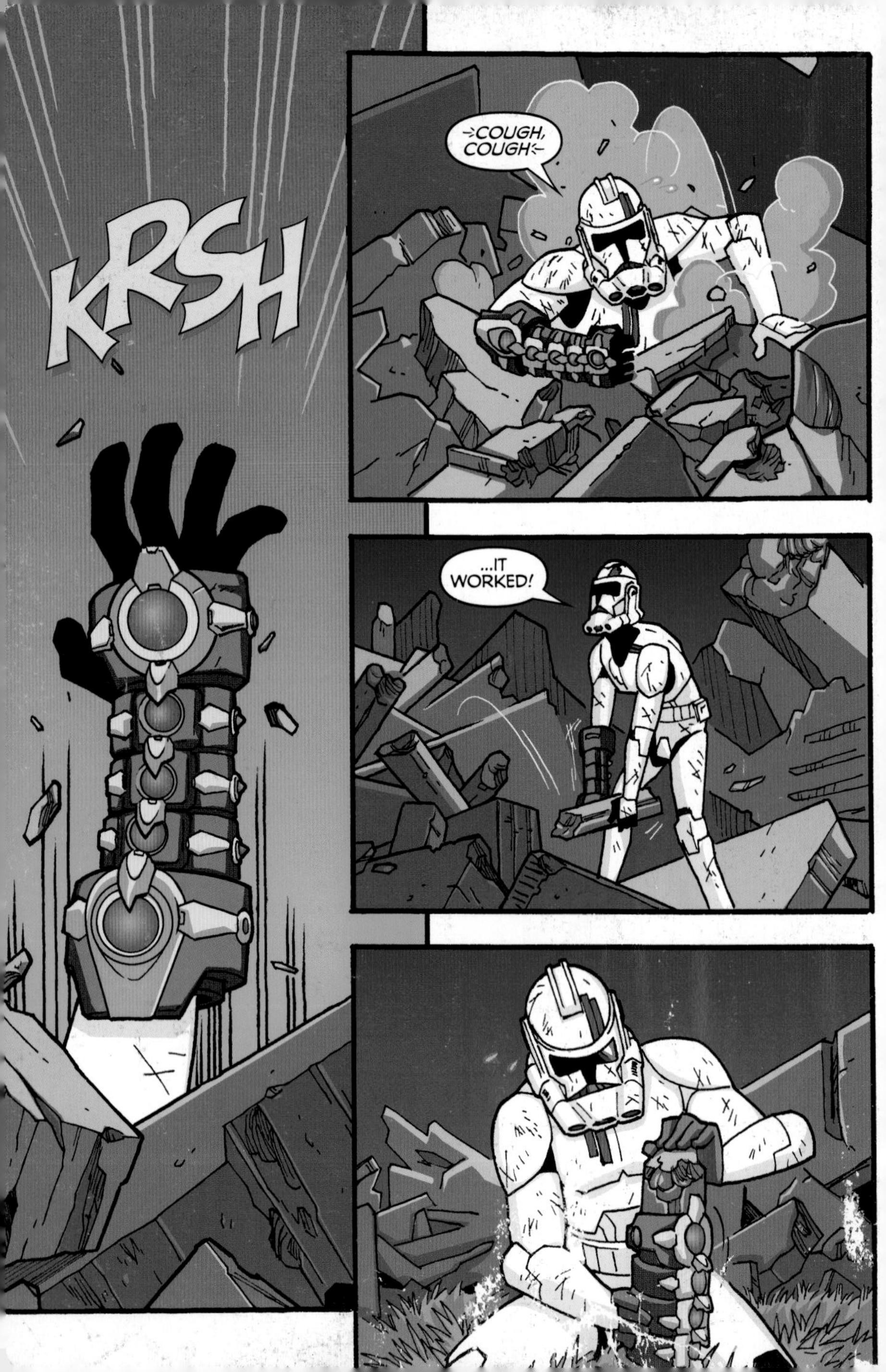
KRSH
-COUGH, COUGH-
...IT WORKED!

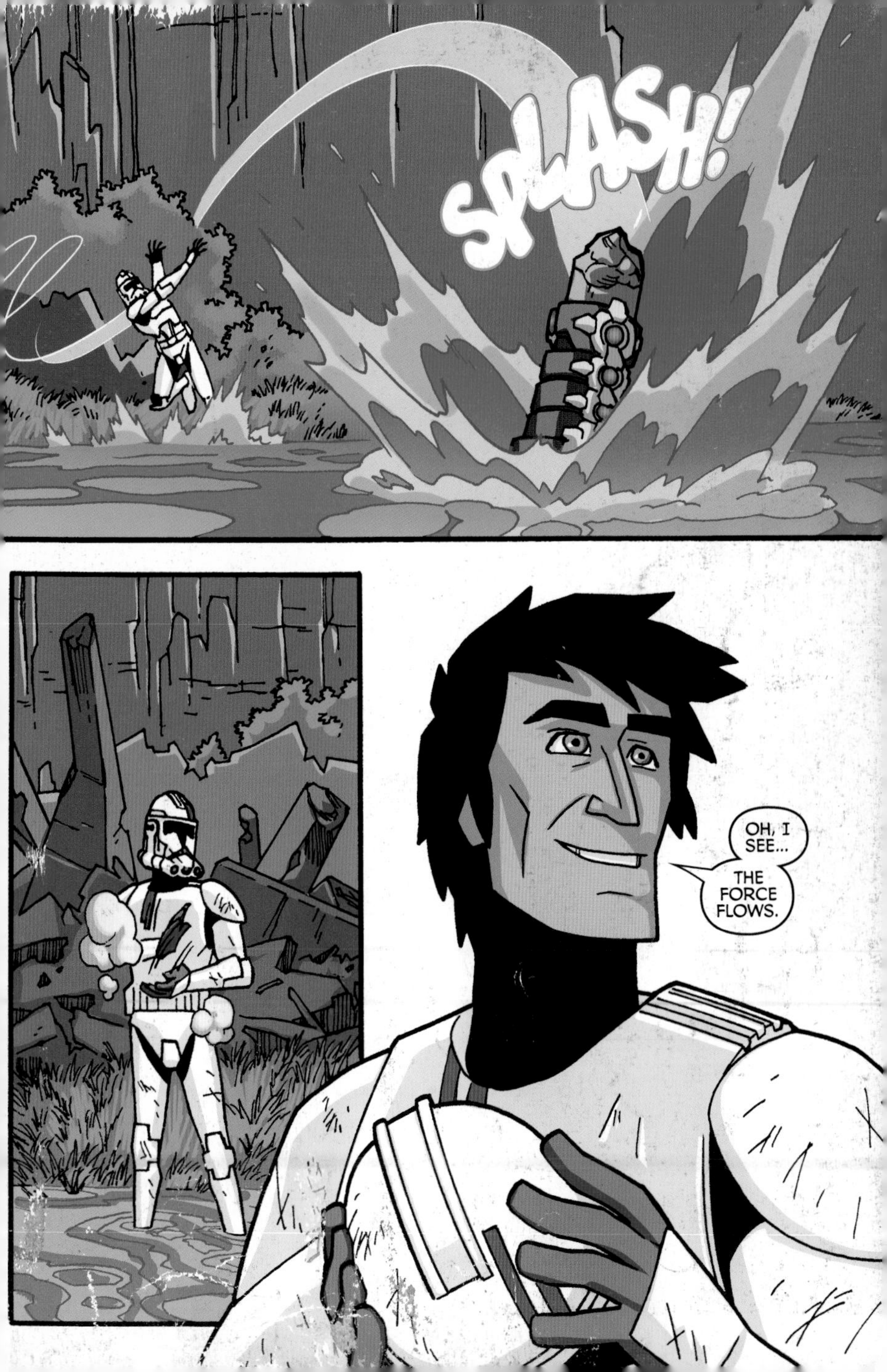
SPLASH!!
OH, I SEE... THE FORCE FLOWS.

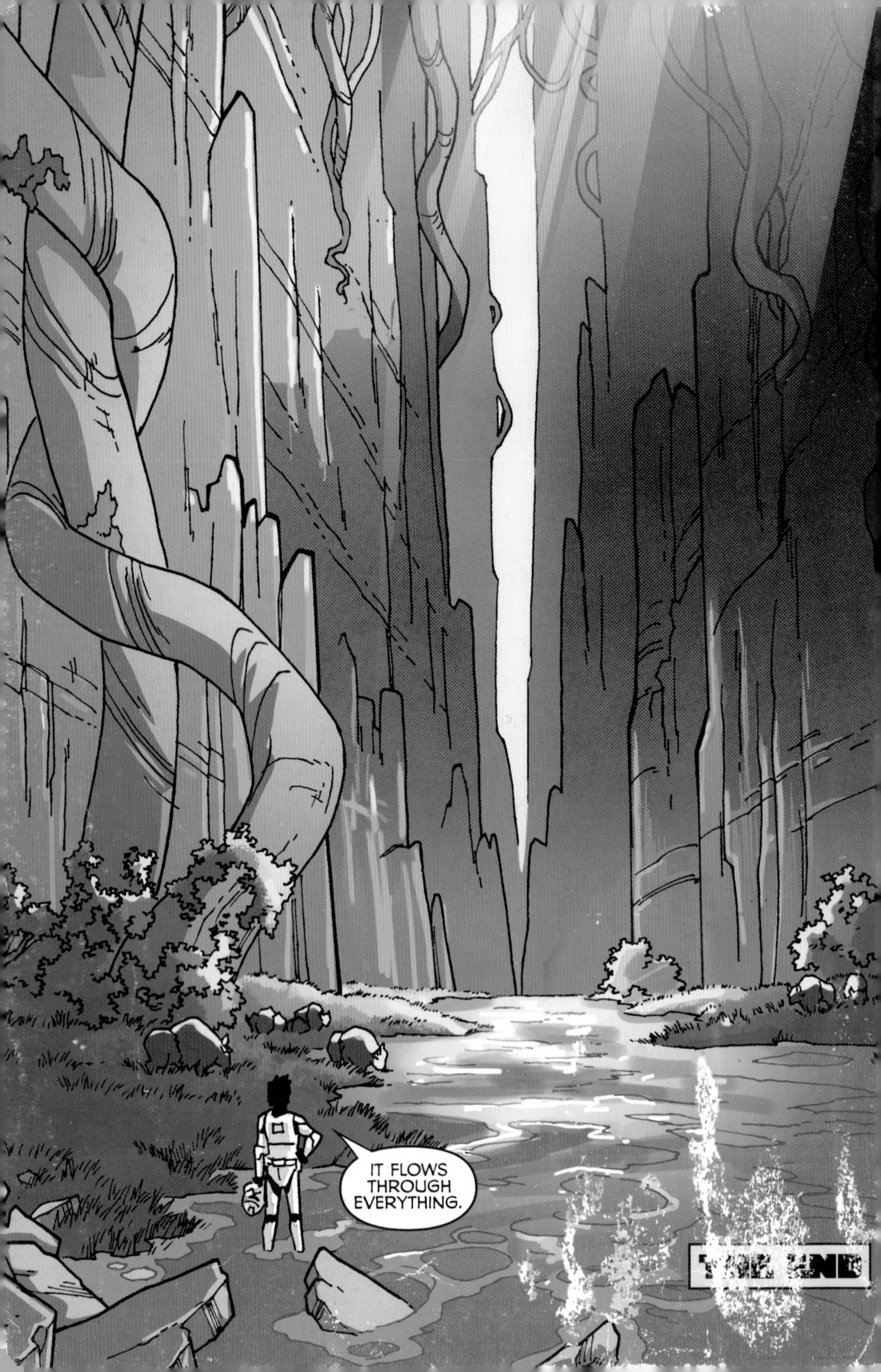
IT FLOWS THROUGH EVERYTHING.
THE END

PRESIDENT AND PUBLISHER **MIKE RICHARDSON**

EXECUTIVE VICE PRESIDENT **NEIL HANKERSON**

CHIEF FINANCIAL OFFICER **TOM WEDDLE**

VICE PRESIDENT OF PUBLISHING **RANDY STRADLEY**

VICE PRESIDENT OF BOOK TRADE SALES **MICHAEL MARTENS**

VICE PRESIDENT OF BUSINESS AFFAIRS **ANITA NELSON**

EDITOR IN CHIEF **SCOTT ALLIE**

VICE PRESIDENT OF MARKETING **MATT PARKINSON**

VICE PRESIDENT OF PRODUCT DEVELOPMENT **DAVID SCROGGY**

VICE PRESIDENT OF INFORMATION TECHNOLOGY **DALE LAFOUNTAIN**

SENIOR DIRECTOR OF PRINT, DESIGN, AND PRODUCTION **DARLENE VOGEL**

GENERAL COUNSEL **KEN LIZZI**

EDITORIAL DIRECTOR **DAVEY ESTRADA**

SENIOR BOOKS EDITOR **CHRIS WARNER**

EXECUTIVE EDITOR **DIANA SCHUTZ**

DIRECTOR OF PRINT AND DEVELOPMENT **CARY GRAZZINI**

ART DIRECTOR **LIA RIBACCHI**

DIRECTOR OF SCHEDULING **CARA NIECE**

DIRECTOR OF INTERNATIONAL LICENSING **TIM WIESCH**

DIRECTOR OF DIGITAL PUBLISHING **MARK BERNARDI**

STAR WARS GRAPHIC NOVEL TIMELINE (IN YEARS)

Omnibus: Tales of the Jedi—5,000–3,986 BSW4

Knights of the Old Republic—3,964–3,963 BSW4

The Old Republic—3653, 3678 BSW4

Knight Errant—1,032 BSW4

Jedi vs. Sith—1,000 BSW4

Omnibus: Rise of the Sith—33 BSW4

Episode I: The Phantom Menace—32 BSW4

Omnibus: Emissaries and Assassins—32 BSW4

Omnibus: Quinlan Vos—Jedi in Darkness—31–30 BSW4

Omnibus: Menace Revealed—31–22 BSW4

Honor and Duty—22 BSW4

Blood Ties—22 BSW4

Episode II: Attack of the Clones—22 BSW4

Clone Wars—22–19 BSW4

Clone Wars Adventures—22–19 BSW4

General Grievous—22–19 BSW4

Episode III: Revenge of the Sith—19 BSW4

Dark Times—19 BSW4

Omnibus: Droids—5.5 BSW4

Omnibus: Boba Fett—3 BSW4–10 ASW4

Omnibus: At War with the Empire—1 BSW4

Episode IV: A New Hope—SW4

Classic Star Wars—0–3 ASW4

Omnibus: A Long Time Ago . . .—0–4 ASW4

Empire—0 ASW4

Omnibus: The Other Sons of Tatooine—0 ASW4

Omnibus: Early Victories—0–3 ASW4

Jabba the Hutt: The Art of the Deal—1 ASW4

Episode V: The Empire Strikes Back—3 ASW4

Omnibus: Shadows of the Empire—3.5–4.5 ASW4

Episode VI: Return of the Jedi—4 ASW4

Omnibus: X-Wing Rogue Squadron—4–5 ASW4

Heir to the Empire—9 ASW4

Dark Force Rising—9 ASW4

The Last Command—9 ASW4

Dark Empire—10 ASW4

Crimson Empire—11 ASW4

Jedi Academy: Leviathan—12 ASW4

Union—19 ASW4

Chewbacca—25 ASW4

Invasion—25 ASW4

Legacy—130–137 ASW4

Old Republic Era
25,000 – 1000 years before
Star Wars: A New Hope

Rise of the Empire Era
1000 – 0 years before
Star Wars: A New Hope

Rebellion Era
0 – 5 years after
Star Wars: A New Hope

New Republic Era
5 – 25 years after
Star Wars: A New Hope

New Jedi Order Era
25+ years after
Star Wars: A New Hope

Legacy Era
130+ years after
Star Wars: A New Hope

Infinities
Does not apply to timeline

Sergio Aragones Stomps Star Wars
Star Wars Tales
Infinities
Tag and Bink
Star Wars Visionaries

BSW4 = before *Episode IV: A New Hope*. ASW4 = after *Episode IV: A New Hope*.

FOR MORE ADVENTURE IN A GALAXY FAR, FAR, AWAY . . .

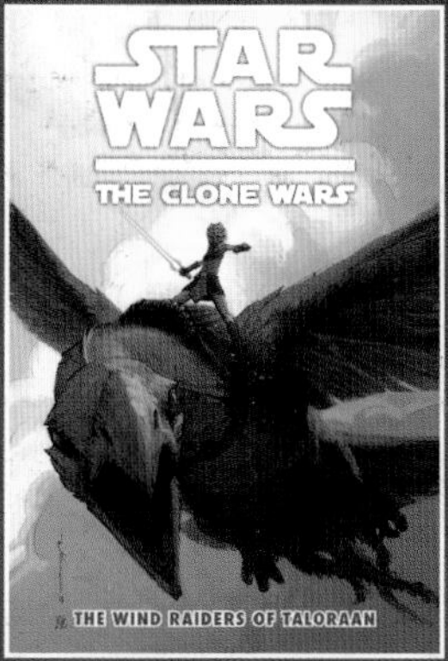
STAR WARS
THE CLONE WARS
THE WIND RAIDERS OF TALORAAN

STAR WARS: THE CLONE WARS—THE WIND RAIDERS OF TALORAAN
978-1-59582-231-4 | $7.99

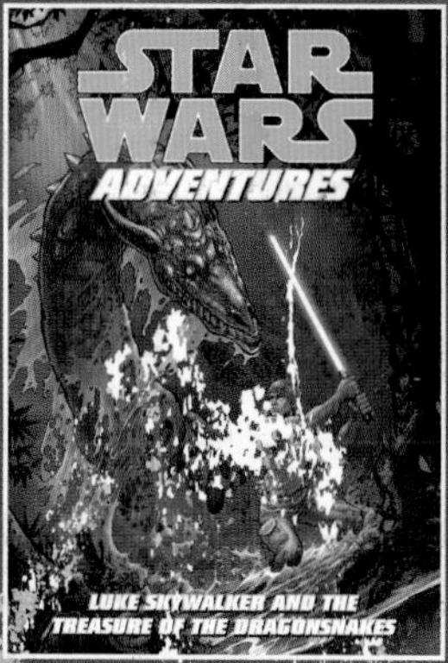
STAR WARS
ADVENTURES
LUKE SKYWALKER AND THE TREASURE OF THE DRAGONSNAKES

STAR WARS ADVENTURES: LUKE SKYWALKER AND THE TREASURE OF THE DRAGONSNAKES
978-1-59582-347-2 | $7.99

STAR WARS ADVENTURES: HAN SOLO AND THE HOLLOW MOON OF KHORYA
978-1-59582-198-0 | $7.99

STAR WARS ADVENTURES: PRINCESS LEIA AND THE ROYAL RANSOM
978-1-59582-147-8 | $7.99

STAR WARS ADVENTURES: THE WILL OF DARTH VADER
978-1-59582-435-6 | $7.99

STAR WARS ADVENTURES: BOBA FETT AND THE SHIP OF FEAR
978-1-59582-436-3 | $7.99

STAR WARS: THE CLONE WARS—SHIPYARDS OF DOOM
978-1-59582-207-9 | $7.99

STAR WARS: THE CLONE WARS—CRASH COURSE
978-1-59582-230-7 | $7.99

STAR WARS: THE CLONE WARS—SLAVES OF THE REPUBLIC
978-1-59582-349-6 | $9.99

STAR WARS: THE CLONE WARS—THE COLOSSUS OF DESTINY
978-1-59582-416-5 | $7.99

STAR WARS: THE CLONE WARS—IN SERVICE OF THE REPUBLIC
978-1-59582-487-5 | $7.99

STAR WARS: THE CLONE WARS—HERO OF THE CONFEDERACY
978-1-59582-552-0 | $7.99

STAR WARS: THE CLONE WARS—DEADLY HANDS OF SHON-JU
978-1-59582-545-2 | $7.99

STAR WARS: THE CLONE WARS—THE ENEMY WITHIN
978-1-59582-845-3 | $7.99

STAR WARS: THE CLONE WARS—THE SITH HUNTERS
978-1-59582-949-8 | $7.99

AVAILABLE AT YOUR LOCAL COMICS SHOP OR BOOKSTORE

To find a comics shop in your area, call 1-888-266-4226
For more information or to order direct: • On the web: darkhorse.com • E-mail: mailorder@darkhorse.com
Phone: 1-800-8[illegible]0052 Mon.–Fri. 9 AM to [illegible] PM Pacific Time.

DARK HORSE BOOKS
darkhorse.com

STAR WARS®

CLONE WARS ADVENTURES

**Don't miss any of the action-packed adventures of your favorite STAR WARS®
characters, available at comics shops and bookstores in a galaxy near you!**

$6.99 each!